Instagram Marketing

Unlock the Secrets to Using this Social Media Platform for Personal Branding, Growing Your Small Business and Connecting with Influencers Who Will Grow Your Brand

Contents

Introduction

Instagram today is more than a few images of your trip or the delicious breakfast you had this morning, and much more than a couple of likes. It's about producing quality content to catch users' attention; recruiting undiscovered talent; buying and selling products; and a platform to voice your opinions and support causes. More importantly, now is the right time to use this resourceful medium for your business, to get the maximum recognition. In fact, Instagram marketing has been so successful recently that it has beaten the quintessential TV commercials, because the market is digitally active and tech-driven now.

If you're here because you need help in marketing your brand on Instagram, you're in the right place. This book contains all the latest information, significant stats and data, up-to-date advice, and a few personal insights that could turn this entertainment platform into a money-making asset.

Since every person and their dog seems to be on Instagram now, why aren't you? Even though it might seem like an insignificant move at the moment, trust us, it's worth the effort. We've seen brands and businesses blooming on this platform that wouldn't have such a massive fan following or customer base otherwise. It really is the biggest marketing boon in today's digital world. And if you're just a beginner, feeling like a child lost in the woods, this book is here to guide you. From the very basics of signing up on Instagram and setting up your profile, to mastering advanced marketing strategies, these chapters will provide you with valuable insights into gaining followers, turning clicks to leads, and driving sales.

If you're thinking of jumping on the Instagram marketing bandwagon this year, this is a great place to start. With around 1 billion active users on this platform—33% of whom are shopping and purchasing products—now is the time to capitalize on this trend. You have an amazing opportunity to make great sales by following the advice presented to you in this book.

There are a lot of businesses today that are using Instagram to promote their brands and make sales, but not all are successful. This platform contains some obscure aspects that need to be acknowledged if you want your campaigns to reach their full potential.

You'll also learn how this social media platform works, how your business can benefit from it, how to use its features (new and old) to create mind-boggling content, how to reach potential customers, and convince users to buy your products or services, and keep them engaged. You'll also find a few secret tactics to help you to stay ahead of every other brand in your discipline, as well as some predictions that are highly likely to turn into trends this year.

If you want to understand these factors and their benefits in detail and make your brand name a huge success, then you've picked up the right book. With the accurate information and reliable resources, you'll be ready to win the Instagram marketing game this year.

PART 1: INSTAGRAM ESSENTIALS

Chapter 1: The Basics of Instagram

Before discussing Instagram for marketing, you first need to know what Instagram is. When this social medium was first introduced in October 2010 by Kevin Systrom and Mike Krieger, no one knew its potential to be one of the top online platforms by the year 2020. Jumping from 100 million users to around 1 billion users, Instagram has gained massive popularity over the last five to six years. Two years after its initial release, Instagram was bought by Facebook for a whopping $1 billion.

As you probably know already, Instagram is basically a social networking app that lets you upload images, videos, GIFs, and stories, at no cost. Users of this app are now amusingly called "Instagrammers." It was initially used to share images of day-to-day life—like breakfast and other meals, vacations, and important moments. Witnessing the massive impact that it had on global users, it was slowly molded into a platform that recognized talent and promoted businesses creatively.

If you're thinking of tapping into this platform and using it for business purposes, you first need to know its basics. Even if you are familiar with it, we'd recommend taking a look at some features that you might have missed.

Creating an Account

The best way to access Instagram is through its mobile application. Once you download it, click on "Sign Up" to create an account by registering with your email ID and a strong password, or by signing up with your Facebook account.

Setting up Your Profile

Next, you'll need to carry out a few steps to set up and complete your profile.

First, you need to think of your username. This is important because you'll be known and recognized by your username or "handle," across the platform. Think outside the box to gain recognition. Whether it's for business or personal use, consider your purpose when joining Instagram, and name your account accordingly. Then, you'll add your profile picture. To do this, find a white circle on your profile where you can add it. You can, of course, change it whenever you want to.

The next step is writing your "bio." You are given 150 characters to describe yourself or what you do, which will be displayed on your profile. You can also mention your real name on your profile, against your creative handle, and add a website link. Now that you have set up your profile and are good to go, it's time to follow friends, family, or other significant people on this platform. You have the "Find Friends" option for already-connected friends through Twitter and Facebook. You can also check the "Discovery" tab that'll show you content according to your preferences.

Uploading Images and Videos

Now, one of the main reasons that you're on Instagram is to share your content with the world. Instagram supports images and video content that will stay on your profile. It's basically a portfolio of your personal life or business. To upload content, you can tap the button of a plus [+] icon and click a picture, or record a video, to share it on the go, or upload an image or video from your phone gallery.

Uploading Images

Initially, Instagram only allowed you to upload images in the square format, which created a lot of restrictions for serious users and content generators. Lately, it has rolled out the feature of uploading images in portrait and landscape modes as well, lifting all restrictions and giving you the freedom to generate content according to your requirements. However, it can still get a bit difficult to determine the correct aspect ratio. This can be solved by clicking on the icon that appears on the bottom-left corner that automatically adjusts the aspect ratio for you. We'd recommend shooting and uploading portrait content more often than landscape, as Instagram is designed to be vertically-oriented.

The platform allows you to upload up to ten images per post, which can be viewed by swiping left. You can also choose the order in which you want your photos to be seen. A lot of people use this feature creatively to show their content in detail.

Filters for Images

After clicking a picture or selecting the image you want to upload, you can click on "Next" and pass your image through a range of filters. There are some amazing ready-to-use filters to vamp up your photographs. If you prefer to edit your image manually, you have tons of options, too. You can crop, change the brightness and saturation, give it a boost, or adjust the sharpness, among many other editing options available.

A lot of users who prefer keeping their photographs professional or who are conducting business through this medium use editing tools such as Aviary, VSCO, and Filmborn. We'd also recommend using any of these tools to make your images and profile stand out.

Uploading Videos

Instagram provides noteworthy options while uploading a video. However, you can only upload a video ranging from between 3 and 60 seconds in length. This is when IGTV videos come to your rescue, about which we'll talk later in this chapter. For the video upload, you can either clip a few shots and edit them together, or cut the video's length as per your preference. Finally, you can choose a cover for your video that'll be seen on your profile when someone visits it. This can be chosen from any moment in your video. An additional benefit while uploading videos is that you can turn off the sound if you don't want it to be heard.

Captions and Tags

Once your image or video is ready with its filters or edits, the last step would be to add a caption, and tag any relevant people in your content. Adding a caption to every post supports your content. However, you're only allowed to put up one caption for an album or a post of multiple images. You can also add the location to every post.

Sharing Posts

Once you're done with the last step, tap on the "Share on Facebook" option if you want to. Finally, tap on "Share" to upload your post. Once the post is uploaded, you can also edit your caption or tag more people by tapping on the "Edit" option.

Notifications

Your notifications can be checked in the fourth category along the bottom of the screen, denoted by a heart icon, located beside the central "plus" icon. You can check the number of likes and comments on your post through this notification panel after you've uploaded any content. If your account is private, other users can send you a follow request, which can also be seen on this panel.

Your Feed

Once you start following certain accounts, their posts will appear on your main feed when you open the app. You can like posts by tapping the heart icon below them or by double-tapping on the image. There's a bubble icon that can be used to comment on people's posts.

Mentions

You can mention other people or your followers in comments by typing "@" followed by their usernames. You can do this on your own posts, as well as on other users' posts. Your friends or followers can mention your name, too. You'll get the update through your notification panel. If you "like" the comment or reply to it, the commenter will be notified as well, possibly starting a conversation thread below the post. Other users can also join the thread.

Apart from these, you will also be notified about the posts that you've liked through the hashtags that you follow.

Stories

The (almost) new sensation of Instagram, the feature of "stories," was initially introduced by Snapchat. It was then applied to Instagram, Facebook, WhatsApp, and now YouTube. Surprisingly, this feature was a major success on Instagram. Stories are highly engaging and interactive, and they play the role of light content that disappears after

24 hours. Also, stories are designed to be vertically formatted, making it utterly comfortable for mobile users to access and engage with them.

To upload a "story," go to your Instagram home page and click on the camera icon that is located in the top-left corner. Take a picture or a selfie, or record a video. You can also upload a picture or video from your gallery. You can add text, filters, hashtags, stickers, emojis, music, and GIFs to make your content playful. A lot of filters and font varieties are available to make your stories more creative. You can also tag or mention people on your stories, or even put the current location, hour, and temperature.

Additional Features

Instagram also introduced the poll feature, where you can ask your followers to choose one option out of the given two. This allows you to swipe through a sliding poll to rate your answer on a scale of 1 to 10. Another interesting and interactive addition is the "Ask me a question" feature, where your followers can ask you a question or reply to yours.

One interesting feature within stories that have encouraged all the millennials and the Gen Z crowd to become engaged is "boomerangs." This feature allows you to create a short video clip that goes backwards and forwards on a loop. It is highly interactive and has been in frequent use since its introduction. The use of augmented reality through filters and lenses has also held the attention of this audience.

Posting Stories

To post your stories, add in all the features you want to use and tap on the "Add to Your Story" option. You can view the list of people who watched your story by tapping on it and clicking on the number of views shown. If you want to hide your story from certain followers, you can go to your story settings and click on "Hide from People." A good alternative is to create a closed group where you can select a few friends that you wish to share your stories with, and it is denoted by a green circle.

To view the stories, you can tap on the pink circle that surrounds a user's profile picture. You can react to their stories through direct emojis or by tapping on the "Reply" option.

IGTV Videos

When they were first introduced, Instagram TV (IGTV) videos didn't get the expected response. These allow users to create videos longer than 60 seconds and up to an hour, and present them in a vertical format to fit phone screens. The latest updates also allow you to post IGTV videos in the landscape format. When you watch a video on the main feed that is more than 60 seconds in length, it'll show you the "Continue Watching" option. This will direct you to the IGTV format, and you can watch the entire video in its designated format. One recent update from Instagram has prompted it to delete the IGTV icon that rested in the top-righthand corner of the app before.

Explore Tab

Instagram's algorithm functions according to your surfing and search results. If you've shown interest in certain topics or viewed posts or videos in a particular category, Instagram will categorize those topics for you and show you relevant content. For instance, if you've searched for fitness, home décor, travel, and recipes, your "Explore" tab (which is the second icon on the bottom panel) will show you those categories and relevant posts that you would like. It gives you a chance to discover accounts you may be interested in.

Direct Messages

Direct messages, or DMs, allow you to send posts to your friends and followers. It is denoted by the arrow button at the bottom of every post. You can also start a conversation within the messages panel. If you aren't following people who are following you, their DMs will reach you in the form of "Requests." It's up to you whether you want to allow the conversation or not. DMs are a great way to conduct interaction.

Other Features

Tags and Photos of You

This is when your friends or followers tag you in their posts. When you visit your profile, you'll notice three icons. The first one is to view your photos in thumbnails of 3x3. The second icon "Posts" lets you see all of your posts as photo tiles that you can scroll through. The fourth icon "Tagged" will show the pictures and videos in which you have been tagged by other users. You can remove the tag from the post and hide it if you don't want it to be seen on your profile. You can also view your followers' tagged pictures by visiting their profiles.

You can tag your friends in a post while preparing it for upload. Click on the option for tagging, tap on your post, and type your friend's username. When the post is uploaded, you can check the tag by tapping the image and clicking on it.

Hashtags

When you're writing your caption before posting any image or video, you can add up to 30 hashtags to boost your profile. Hashtags allow your posts to be seen and discovered by other users because popular hashtags are categorized in a different album within the "Explore" bar. It gives the users who are searching for content within your niche the opportunity to explore your profile. A useful Instagram feature is that you can simply type "#," and you'll be provided with popular hashtags within your category. Still, be sure to stay relevant and use specific hashtags to target your audience. You can also follow certain hashtags that will appear in your feed from various accounts that frequently use and post their content with that hashtag.

Multiple Accounts

This amazing feature, which was introduced in February 2016, lets you use multiple accounts. Offering you the advantage of creating and switching up to five accounts simultaneously, this feature is beneficial to those who want to keep their personal and professional portfolios separate. To create a new account, you can go to your profile and tap on settings. You'll find an "Add an Account" option. Click on it to repeat the process to create more accounts. When you visit your profile, you'll get an option to switch between your active accounts through an arrowed list.

Instagram Live

This feature is extremely useful for "influencers" and people who want to create engagement with their followers. Instagram Live lets you record videos of live events and happenings in real-time. Your viewers can also interact with you through comments and likes, letting you know about their opinions or questions.

Instagram Web

The web version of this platform, instagram.com, can also be used as the web version on any device. Since it doesn't allow uploading any content, most users prefer using the app version. It doesn't provide any additional benefits apart from getting embed codes.

Account Privacy

Lastly, if you want your content to be seen and discovered all over the world, go to your account settings through your profile, click on "Privacy" > "Account Privacy," and turn off the "Private Account" option. This will give you a chance to showcase your portfolio to the world and increase your chances of being recognized sooner.

These are the basics that you need to know if you're new to this social media platform and before using Instagram for marketing. There are still a few minute features that you need to learn about, which we'll discuss in the upcoming chapters. In the next chapter, we'll go through the benefits of using Instagram for business and marketing.

Chapter 2: Why Use Instagram for Your Business

When we get bored, the first thing that most of us do is pick up our phones and tap on Instagram. This social media platform has become such a common part of our daily lives that most brands and marketers are making complete use of this fact, building their brand identity through this free and useful tool. Instagram has proven to be one of the top and most successful platforms to drive sales and create maximum brand awareness.

As we discussed previously, Instagram has had a massive leap in the number of followers who use this platform for personal, creative, and professional purposes. Lately, a lot of brands have made Instagram their primary tool to drive their businesses. There's so much to explore and create. It has provided the freedom of advertising and content generation like never before. If your business hasn't been on Instagram until now, it's high time you got into it and started to create ways to mark your online presence. To be recognized in this digitally centered world, Instagram can be your way out.

Apart from this, there are several other reasons why it's absolutely important to tap into this marketing arena this year.

One Billion Users

Boasting a total of one billion active users to date, this social media platform has no foreseeable lack of customers. With a huge number of millennials and Gen Z using this platform for leisure, you can target the majority of the younger audience if your brand demands it, especially since 38% of the total users tend to open and check Instagram multiple times in a day. With so much traffic and viewers that immensely appreciate and accept new ideas and creativity, you can map a lot of customers through this platform.

Target Your Audience Group

Widely used around the globe and by almost all age groups, Instagram is the perfect platform to form and target your audience group. According to an analysis by Statista, the USA has the most users, followed by India and Brazil, Indonesia, and Russia. It is rapidly growing in the United Kingdom and Canada, as well.

An important aspect of Instagram marketing and your target audience is your reach. Even if you have brilliant content and a defined target audience, you won't drive more sales or increase engagement if you cannot reach more people. To reach more users based on their countries, you can tap into the five countries that have the highest reach percentages, which are Brunei, Iceland, Turkey, Sweden, and Kuwait.

As for age and gender, the major age group that is active on Instagram ranges from 18 to 29, which makes up around 67% of all users. This is followed by the age group 30 - 49, which is 47%, and 50 - 64, which is 23%. The age group of 65+ constitutes 8% of active users on Instagram. The gender ratio, on the other hand, is almost even on this platform, with 48% males and 52% females.

All these factors—age, gender, nationality, and the number of active users on a daily basis—make up your target audience. You need to define your group and play your content and marketing strategies accordingly.

Interaction Made Easy

Once you've mapped your target audience, you can plan your content accordingly and develop strategies to grab their attention. The best way of doing this is to create engaging content that inspires them to interact with your brand. A big chunk of followers is tempted to check out brand products and buy them if they feel at ease or develop trust.

Live videos have made interaction super fun for customers and brands, giving them the opportunity to communicate with brand faces and team members in real-time conversations. It makes them feel more attached to your brand and drives more sales. Stories are another way to create engagement; you can request answers through polls, do a question and answer (Q&A) session, or ask specific questions to your target audience. Since around 500 million users post and watch stories on a daily basis, one-third of which are from businesses, there's a higher chance of gaining more followers if your content is promising.

Brands also request customers to tag and mention their friends to win hampers, trips, or certain products. This further helps to gain more interaction and potential customers.

Freedom to Create Various Types of Content

Initially, based on the concept of images, Instagram was actually about portraying your everyday life and showing off your photography skills. Later on, it was slowly converted into a marketing tool. This is because people are more drawn to visual content that is aesthetically pleasing and easy to decipher. Let's see how the three main types of content on Instagram—images, text, and videos—help to get other users' attention.

Images

Images are arguably the best form of visual marketing, and Instagram is the best place to create interaction based on images and photographs. Also, if your business requires putting up more images to showcase your products and support a cause, you're approaching the right medium. This creates your brand's personality and keeps your followers engaged. Creating edited photographs or making collages to present your products or your concept are the most common ways of using images for marketing.

Text

To begin marketing on Instagram, you first need to define whether your brand is visual or not, depending on the concept, products, and brand language you want to create. Even though text might not have the same impact as visual content, you can still incorporate it onto images or write powerful captions to support your style. Also, hashtags count as a type of written content that helps in creating recognition within your niche.

Videos

Video engagement has massively increased in popularity recently. Content creators are looking for creative ways of incorporating their products into short videos that can grab their followers' attention. It can be product reviews, crossovers, interviews, or DIY projects. This type of content is more engaging for almost all followers, and they tend to watch the entire video.

As we have discussed before, the use of stories and IGTV videos is the new sensation among Instagram marketers, content creators, and brands. According to an Ispos survey in 2019, 62% of Instagram and other similar app users aged between 13 - 54 claimed they are more interested in buying a product from any brand after they've noticed it on stories.

The Benefits of Hiring Influencers

The new-age way of presenting your products or your brand face, influencer marketing, is a top-notch tactic that most of the brands use today. Influencers are like mini-celebrities on social media platforms who have a massive following and a great impact on their followers. Brands are realizing the potential of this influence and rapidly hiring influencers to promote their products. Specific benefits of doing so include:

Reaching a Massive Target Group

People appreciate and follow various influencers due to their personal style and consistency. This has helped influencers to develop a specific audience that follows their advice and tips. You need to approach such influencers who are aligned with your product style and have a massive impact on your target audience. For instance, if you're selling skincare products or cosmetics, it can help to hire a makeup artist or a fashion blogger who has a majority of followers that are interested in these topics.

Presenting Your Products in Creative Ways

At times, brands and marketers get saturated and face creative blocks in presenting their products and services. There's so much creativity and so many cutting-edge advertising ideas on social media today that it can get difficult to compete in the market. This is the point where hiring influencers can come to your rescue. These people have built their own language in communicating with their audience, which can be completely different from your content. This can give your products a fresh feel and look, as well.

Proper Budget Planning

Influencers on social media are paid an amount that ranges from $100 to $2,085 for a single image, $114 to $3,138 for videos, and $43 to $721 for stories, depending on their reach and number of followers. Even though it might sound like a lot, these numbers are actually useful in budget planning and cost-cutting. This strategy has been such a huge success, particularly on Instagram, that brands and content marketers in the US have set a specific budget of 69% for influencers who have been successful on this social media platform. So, influencers can prove to be game-changers in driving sales for your company, making them an asset for an effective return of investment.

The Power of Advertising

Instagram holds the massive power of reaching up to 849.3 million users among the one billion active users, with 52.9 million of those falling into the young age group. This creates a major impact on advertising and sales. This social media platform has also introduced extended tools for advertising. Brands can pay a certain amount of money to this platform to showcase their ads or relevant content.

It ultimately aims at getting more views, driving more traffic to the website or mobile application, and creating more brand awareness. Marketers are allocating a part of their budget for advertising content as it has lately been a successful tactic.

Video Ads

While scrolling through your Instagram feed, you must have come across a lot of videos that have the label "Sponsored" on top of them. These video ads are paid for by the brands, and Instagram shows them to users who have a search history related to the respective fields. This increases your chances of selling your products and getting more followers.

Photo Ads

Similar to sponsored video ads, photo ads are single images that show the product or concept. An additional "Learn More" button directs the users to the brand's page.

Carousel Ads

An updated version of photo ads, carousel ads consist of multiple images that can be swiped through to learn more about the product or concept in detail.

Story Ads

You can also create ads on your stories about important dates, events, and new launches, with a "Swipe-up" feature that will lead your followers to your website for further information.

Selling Your Products

With its recently integrated shopping tools, Instagram is a fun and convenient way to shop for most of your favorite products. While 81% of all users depend on Instagram to search for old and new products, 11% of users from the United States exclusively buy from this platform now. It shows even greater potential for expansion this year.

Speaking of Instagram's shopping tools, you can access this feature through a business account. By adding multiple products to an image, you can have your followers tap on it to fetch details about each. It also lets them check out for payment without directing them to a new website or page. This feature has been a hit among the majority of the users due to its convenience. You can also access the "Shop Now" feature that can encourage your customers to at least check out the products.

Users are also tapping into this social media platform to buy new products based on word-of-mouth recommendations or simply upon noticing the quality that is offered. This can give you a massive opportunity to generate revenue and drive more sales than anticipated.

Use of a Business Account

You can take the maximum advantage of using a business account on Instagram while promoting your brand. This feature was introduced in 2016 and has been used by brands and marketing companies ever since to drive insights and compare analytical data. It shows the age group, gender, and nationality of people who have interacted with your posts. This helps in analyzing your content according to the number of likes, comments, shares, and saved posts, and lets you change or tweak it for the next marketing plan to get more interaction. It also shows the analysis of interaction garnered during every day of the week and at particular hours, giving you insight into the right time to post. Basically, all these demographics can entirely change your content strategy and for good.

Even though we will discuss the benefits of using a business profile in detail in the next chapter, a brief highlight would make its importance clearer. It helps you use important information such as contact information and website links, which are very important for any business. You can also promote and advertise your content.

A Creative Way to Portray Your Brand

Before the onset of social media marketing, we never knew that certain brands and companies had a lighter side to them. Sure, there were TV commercials, but those were solely commercial and did not aim at interaction or engagement. Instagram marketing has led users to believe that there are humans behind the top brands. With lighter content like behind-the-scenes videos and team interviews, consumers are able to see the legitimate side of brands and are able to trust them more. Earlier in this chapter, we also talked about how influencers can promote your products or business with a creative edge. You can also use extreme tactics such as holding contests or giving shout-outs.

Instagram offers multiple tools and an aesthetically pleasing theme to unleash your creativity and show any kind of content you want. Your brand will have a target audience that can be lured with content that they wish to see. This social media platform offers you support and a blank canvas to put out your portfolio. The only challenge is to create your own style and brand personality. But once you do it, you're bound to stand out and get recognition. Also, it's completely easy to use this tool, making it suitable for beginners.

Even though this medium has a lot of potential and functionality when it comes to promoting your business, it is getting extremely saturated and competitive. However, it doesn't seem likely to lose its potential any time soon. Since it is designed to be mobile-friendly, this aspect allows users to access the brand's content and products on the go, increasing the chances of interaction and sales. We highly recommend that you build and promote your brand on Instagram this year to gain maximum benefit from the new features and sales tools.

Chapter 3: Instagram Challenges and Changes

While using Instagram is a fun and effective way of marketing and promoting your business, there are a few challenges and limitations that marketers have been facing over the years. It might seem dainty and glittery on the outside, but this social media platform has its own flaws, too. Even though these cannot be deemed as disadvantages, being aware of the limitations can help you plan your content and marketing strategy accordingly.

And while these challenges remain, Instagram has been working on a number of new features, some of which are already being tested in a few regions. They could either work to your advantage or completely change your marketing game.

As you're planning to jump on the Instagram bandwagon this year, we'd recommend tracking the challenges and changes that you could possibly face on this social media platform.

Challenges Related to Instagram

People who use Instagram to display their professional work and business owners who promote their content to potential customers have been facing certain limitations since the onset of this medium.

We're pointing out some of the major challenges related to it for you to be prepared and plan your strategies accordingly.

Web Version Isn't Optimized

Originally designed to be more functional as a mobile application, Instagram hasn't been able to deliver a well-designed and optimized web version until now. Even though we can now view new features like stories on the web version, a few features still aren't available, such as posting images and videos. Also, the images and content, in general, aren't optimized to be viewed properly on all devices. Instagram has fewer features on the website than the mobile application, making the web version less convenient to use.

So, in order to post constantly and to update your brand's Instagram account, you'd need to keep a smartphone or a tablet handy, instead of a desktop computer or a laptop. In this case, it can get difficult to maintain working conditions in an environment that's not mobile-friendly, especially if you don't have a dedicated social media team or department yet.

No Clickable Links in Posts

Writing an effective caption can be difficult, especially when most people prefer to access visual content instead of reading text. A greater challenge with Instagram captions is that they don't support clickable links. You simply cannot expect your followers to copy and paste the link by leaving the Instagram interface, as it is inconvenient.

No one, including you, would want to leave the app and browse another website by copying and pasting the URL unless it is extremely intriguing. We need to spoon-feed every tiny detail to potential customers to expect more sales and interaction. You need to come up with more conventional ideas, such as adding the relevant link to your bio or using shopping tools that can direct your customers to your website or the installation link of your mobile application.

This can be a challenge if your content requires your audience to arrive at a specific landing page with every post, especially if you rely on Instagram for generating revenue and driving sales. It can be a bigger limitation when your target audience is above the age group of

35 or 40, as these users generally aren't technologically advanced compared to the millennials or the Gen Z users.

Certain Downsides of Advertisements

Scrolling through Instagram comes with the downside of watching advertisements and sponsored posts every now and then. Since almost every business is promoting its products and services on this social medium, it has nearly reached a point of saturation. After every few stories and around four to five posts, you can see a sponsored post that is based on your recent search history. Certain advertisements popping up on the main feed get too repetitive at some point.

Among all the ads, a lot of them are fake, too. A few startups simply create false ads and promote them to gain more followers and generate more leads by luring users into freebies or heavy discounts. A lot of users have claimed to have fallen into this trap. It's difficult to differentiate between authentic ads and false ones.

Advertising on Instagram can also turn out to be expensive. It can get a bit difficult to set and manage a budget for ads on this platform, especially if you're just starting out. You need constant cash flow or high funding. Unless you're a huge, established business that can easily set a budget aside for advertising on social media platforms, you'll just have to rely on organic traffic and customers who are genuinely interested in purchasing your products through interaction and high engagement. Since the average CPC (cost per click) on Instagram ranges from $0.50 to $1 (the average being $0.61), it can take some time for you to earn back what you've spent on sponsoring your posts, or at least until you break even.

The costs of advertising vary according to the business or type of brand you own. If you own a company that follows a concept based on technology, you might have to pay higher than those in the entertainment business. There's another downside to paying for advertising. When you switch to a business account, you're provided with free analytics and demographics, but there's a catch here. Instagram often reduces the reach and engagement of your posts to earn money from paid advertising and promotion of posts. This can be a big disadvantage to smaller businesses that are already on a limited budget and need more engagement during their initial days.

Limited Target Audience

Compared to Facebook and Twitter, Instagram has less ability to target local markets. It also creates less visibility and doesn't target a major crowd because Instagram's algorithm functions to promote and update content from personal accounts rather than business accounts. A lot of brands cater to all age groups. And with Instagram, it can get difficult to reach the audience that's beyond the age of 35 as this group only comprises a handful of users. Moreover, your posts will target only 13% of this age group. So, Instagram wouldn't be the best platform to promote your business if your products or services target an older age group.

Even though men constitute 48% of the total users compared to women making up 52%, only 32% of the former are active on Instagram on a monthly basis. This can minimize your reach to potential customers if your products are aimed at men. Even if you're successful in reaching your target audience by a minor margin, most of them would simply like, comment, or share. It's extremely difficult to convert engagement into sales—as liking and sharing are rather simple actions when it comes to revenue generation. Even if a user likes your content, it doesn't necessarily mean that he will like your product enough to buy it or have a meaningful connection with your brand.

Since Instagram is officially only available for Android and iOS, users with devices that run on other operating systems cannot access this platform. Also, not all potential customers have access to or use Instagram. Some users have lately been realizing the addiction that is caused by social media, and are either going on a "social media detox" or uninstalling apps. Still, it is safe to say that these are only a handful of accounts that hardly make any difference in the grand scheme of things.

Lack of Privacy Settings

One of the privacy settings that we all want and are hoping to access in the future is privacy concerning each post. At present, we're unable to make certain posts private and others public according to our preferences. You can only set your entire account to private or public. As for hiding content, you can either archive your posts—and add them back to your profile later if you want—or delete them entirely.

Changes Expected to Occur on the Platform in 2020

While we witnessed major changes in 2019, such as the introduction of dark mode, the "Restrict" feature to block hateful comments, and the countdown timer on stories, among several others, we still have a lot more to look forward to this year and can plan ahead accordingly.

Hiding "Likes" from Posts

In 2019, the platform started testing its new feature of hiding likes on posts in a few countries, including Italy, Australia, and now the United States. Instagram announced it was taking this massive step to reduce comparison and cyberbullying, and make the platform more than just a race for likes. Even though it might affect the engagement and interaction of followers with brands in some ways, the features of commenting, sharing, and interacting through stories and live videos will remain, keeping the engagement intact. Even before the feature rolls out globally, a few brands are already worried about the loss of interaction it could cause. However, it is important to note that you will still be able to view the number of likes that you've received on your posts; it'll just be invisible to other users.

This could lead to a change that all brands could benefit from—the restriction of fake accounts and bots that try to hack handles with more followers or engagement, and take over their genuine content. These changes have been successful in most of the countries they were tried in, and could possibly be introduced to all countries that use Instagram this year. So, we'd suggest planning your marketing and content strategies accordingly.

Insights for Hashtags

Using hashtags has been a common strategy to increase visibility on various social media platforms. Instagram allows you to add up to 30 hashtags to your caption below the post. While a few marketing experts advocate for adding only famous hashtags in order to be seen in the "Explore" feed and be categorized easily within your niche, some suggest creating your own hashtags and experimenting with them. Once your unique hashtag gains traction and gets recognized easily, it helps to create brand awareness and mark brand identity.

A recent feature with the hashtags suggests the number of impressions that every hashtag provides you. It helps you understand the use of individual tags and gives you a clear idea of what's working. It is far more useful than the previously collected impressions that would otherwise get difficult to analyze. This feature will assist you in creating a clear plan of captions and hashtags for your future posts and diminish the need for relying on web surfing to chart out popular hashtags. We can expect this feature to be accessible to all users around the world to improve marketing, especially brands and content marketers.

If your Instagram has this feature available, you can view the insights below a new post and take a look at the impressions from hashtags.

Creator Profiles

Along with personal and business accounts, creators such as influencers and bloggers are offered an option called "Creator Profiles." This feature will let such content creators have more control over their "Direct Messages" panel with the ability to sort out their messages, and the choice to follow specific data. To switch to a creator profile, you can open "Settings," tap on "Account," then follow "Switch to Professional Account" > "Creator."

Even though this feature is quite new, we can expect a few tweaks or new updates within the category this year. This is because the community of influencers and bloggers is rapidly growing on social media, and they, too, need a specific type of account to cater to their needs. It'll also help them understand whether the type of content they're producing is attracting enough attention or not.

Story Templates and Interface

The latest updates on this social media platform include adding quizzes, questions and answers, GIFs, and stickers to your stories. You might have also noticed the new story templates that allow you to type answers in those empty boxes, making interaction more fun. This year, we can expect an even better interface that'll allow for more user-friendly templates and interactive features, which will be useful for brands to increase interaction.

You can increase interaction by asking simple questions to your followers, such as "What are the books you're currently reading?" or "Which beauty products do you recommend?" The templates that are developed to provide users with an easy and appealing interface will urge them to answer. We're hoping for more such templates and interfaces in 2020.

Instagram Scheduler

Even though a lot of businesses have been using third-party tools to schedule, update, and upload posts, Instagram has recently launched its native scheduler to help businesses flourish on this platform. However, this feature isn't 100% effective yet, because it has a few limitations. First, you're not allowed to schedule your stories, which form a very important part of marketing and interaction campaigns. Second, you'll have to use Creator Studio instead of using the Instagram app to work with the scheduler. Third, you'll need to link your Facebook page to this scheduler so that it can function.

If you think that you're used to the third-party tool you're currently using, and if it already functions well, you can wait for the new Instagram Scheduler features or updates to make it more efficient. But if you're new to it, you can start by using the Instagram Scheduler and become acquainted with it until the new update rolls in.

Whichever tool you use, for now, just make sure that it saves you time and makes your tasks easier.

Despite these challenges and changes, Instagram is still one of the most sought-after media apps to promote your business organically. Whether it's a company that is a household name or a tiny mom-and-pop shop, every business has seen some form of success on Instagram by using excellent marketing strategies and producing consistent content. Even though it's not all sunshine and rainbows, you can definitely overcome these limitations and carve your path to recognition on this social media platform.

Chapter 4: Setting Up Your Business Profile

While we've already discussed the benefits of using an Instagram business account, this chapter will deal with all the "hows" and "whys" of using it in detail. Here, we will discuss the details of setting up a business account, along with the additional features and benefits that you might have missed in the previous chapter.

Setting Up a Business Account

Set Up Your Profile

You must remember our instructions for setting up an Instagram account at the beginning of this book. Switching to a business account follows a similar path. You first need to sign in and prepare a regular account, after which you can switch the profile to a business account. Let's discuss the initial stage again, this time in more detail, to help you prepare for the switch to a business account.

- Basics

Let's say you're a new user, and you've followed the instructions given in the first chapter to create an account. As we know, you can either sign up with your phone number or email ID and password or use your Facebook login details to link your Instagram account to it.

To start with the basic business account setup, you need to add your professional email ID, contact number, and workplace address if you wish clients to approach you. But filling one contact field is mandatory to complete setting up your profile. We'd suggest using your work email ID as it helps you find professional contacts easily, and vice versa.

- **Choosing the Profile Picture**

Even though Instagram doesn't allow users to view profile pictures in a full-screen mode, it still plays a significant role in your recognition. In fact, it becomes more of a challenge, since the window is only 110x110 pixels, so you need to make sure that you're creating an impact with the tiny display picture. You need to choose your profile picture or "avatar" depending on your business niche and discipline. It can either be your logo or a creative snapshot of your products, depending on the people you want to pursue and your target audience. If you have a lot of personal relationships, you can also use your headshot to make sure that your followers know you and your business.

Nowadays, businesses are competitive and thrive on presenting their best versions online. This is why you can find a lot of creativity put into profile pictures of business accounts, too. This might just convey the importance of having an apt avatar.

- **Writing a Compelling Bio**

Writing your Instagram bio is a creative challenge. You're only given a few characters to work with, and you have to describe your brand or convey your message in a line or two. It needs to be strong, compelling, and descriptive enough for people to be attracted to so that they check out and follow your account. You also need to make sure that the style of writing goes well with your profile's aesthetic theme. Try to add as many relevant keywords as possible to be ranked among the top searches. This is just how Search Engine Optimization and Instagram algorithms work. If you cannot think out of the box, keep the description simple yet informative, as it could backfire otherwise. Your followers should simply know what you do and what your goals are, which is compelling enough.

While you're at it, make sure you add your brand hashtag and website link at the end of your bio for your followers to visit your web page and increase traffic. It shows authenticity and gives a professional edge to your brand.

- **Finding Relevant Contacts to Follow**

If you've connected your account to Facebook while signing up, you will automatically have a list of suggestions for followers from your Facebook friend list. You'll find an "Invite Facebook Friends" option that can be used to send an invitation to your entire friend list. You can also find friends from other social networks such as Gmail, Twitter, Yahoo!, or LinkedIn.

Another option is to find friends and followers manually by tapping on the "Skip for Now" option. You can always go back to searching for friends on Facebook if you need to find relevant contacts. You can search for people or mutual contacts that have been interested in your business. Send them a follow request. It is highly likely that you'll get a follow back from them. Give shout-outs or hold giveaways to request more followers. Keep on trying all methods until you've established a concrete following base that'll organically reach new followers time and again.

We would, however, advise against buying followers to show a high following count on your profile. It's an inorganic reach that'll break at some point and fail to generate revenue. It's better to have a slow start instead and keep on going until you succeed, which you will.

Pick an Appropriate Name

In addition to the above, we've also mentioned the importance of thinking of an apt username for your Instagram account. It matters a lot because this name will be recognized on online platforms that'll make your mark. It is, of course, advisable to stick to your brand's name if you're conducting business on this social media platform, as it'll be the handle that people will use when they're searching for your brand. It should definitely be catchy, but also easy for users to remember so they can search your name whenever they want to.

If your preferred name or handle isn't available, you can find creative ways of fitting your handle in the Instagram pool either by adding punctuation, additions like ".com" or "I am" in the beginning, or "official" at the end of the brand name, depending on your business category. This, along with your profile picture, will show the professional side of your business and help you make a great first impression. For instance, if you're a fashion brand or a garment company named "Bend the Trend," your account handle can be @bendthetrend.official; or if you're working in a real estate agency, you can choose a username that displays your name with your profession, such as "@timgoldberg_realtor" to differentiate your professional account from your personal one. Try to find a username that's close to your brand name by experimenting with different combinations.

You'll also have the option of choosing the title of the page or page category, in which you'll have to mention the discipline that your company is in. A few examples of common categories include art, technology, entertainment, media, movies, music, restaurants, food, sports, fashion, event sources, websites, mobile applications, local businesses, and many others.

Switch to a Business Account

Now that you've created an account that is up and running, it's time to make the switch. Go to your profile, tap on the three horizontal lines on the top-right corner, and tap on "Settings." You'll see the option "Switch to Business Profile." Tap on it and turn it on. You now have access to a lot of useful features that personal accounts don't, such as running ads and viewing engagement analytics. We'll delve further into these features later.

Complete Your Profile

Completing and editing your profile is a must to keep your account fresh and receive more followers each day. If you've already uploaded a suitable profile picture, a good bio, and your website link, it's time to try a few more tactics such as changing your language or adding links to brands and promotions to lure more customers.

- **Connecting Your Facebook Page**

If you already have a Facebook business page, you can now connect it to your Instagram business account to be able to use the business tools. If you don't have a Facebook page yet, you'll need to create one.

Create Your Brand's Aesthetic Theme

An attractive Instagram theme instantly creates a great first impression. If you own a company that sells certain products, you can create aesthetically appealing content surrounding them. One major factor that plays an important role in defining an awesome Instagram feed is the color palette. A lot of successful brands use a lighter or pastel color palette in their images and videos. A few also use grids and collages to make it appealing when users scroll through their feeds. If your feed is engaging, users are bound to open your posts, then like, share, and follow your account.

If you feel that you don't have that creative edge, you can hire freelance graphic designers, photographers, or aspiring art directors that fit your budget. If your products or services don't demand or fit into the "aesthetic" aspect, stick to simplicity, and just stay consistent for your content to be noticed. If it's powerful, you're bound to get more leads. Even though we'll talk about content generation and staying consistent in the upcoming chapter, it's important to make a note of it.

Another underrated point is the use of fonts. If your posts use text that conveys certain messages or product information, it is important to choose appropriate fonts that'll appeal to your audience. It's almost certain that you'll use text on your content at some point. It could be text overlays on images or subtitles on your videos.

Promote Your Posts and Share

Since we'll be talking about the types of content in the next few chapters, for now, we'll directly skip to promoting and sharing your posts after having created and uploaded them. First, make sure you write captivating captions. At times, the strength of captions can lead to more shares than the post itself. Captions have made their way into micro-blogging to share personal stories that followers get attached to. To increase the sharing of your posts, you need to make sure that you increase interaction with your followers by engaging them in stories or simply responding to their comments.

Share your posts on your stories and encourage your followers to share them, too. Further promotion tactics involve paying for sponsored posts and running ads. You can set a budget and spend it on the various types of ads that are provided by Instagram and Facebook. These media will either target the audience depending on their search histories or your existing target audience. We will talk more about ads, their types, and how to use them further in this book.

Why Choose a Business Account Over a Personal or Creator Account?

By now, you have a general idea of what Instagram business account analytics do. They provide insights and demographics related to your followers and what they do. Let's talk about them in more detail now.

So, we already know that the analytics fetch details regarding your followers' age group, location, and gender in the "Audience" category. These are also useful in knowing the interaction and engagement that your followers have had with every post. You can do this by checking the number of likes and comments, as well as the shared and saved posts in the "Activity" panel.

Moreover, a business profile offers the look and feel of a professional brand and sets you apart from normal users. And of course, we have the undeniably important "Promote" and "Sell" tabs to boost your business.

The following questions will encourage you to use Instagram analytics and insights when you begin:

➤ What is the total amount of content that we generated over the past week? Is it more or less than what we had generated previously?

➤ Are these posts enough to drive the required engagement?

➤ Who are our followers, and where are they from?

➤ How many profile views, impressions, and website clicks did we generate over the past month?

➤ What is the age group and gender of our target audience?

➤ Which days of the week bring us the highest engagement? What are the peak hours that most users interact with our posts?

➤ How many users are more interested in stories than posts?

Contemplating these questions and their answers can automatically derive a marketing and content strategy plan. You'll be clear on who your audience is and what your followers like, which is often very difficult for beginners to decipher. Create a marketing plan accordingly and keep on making necessary changes according to your data insights and analytics.

Additional Factors

We've clearly understood the important benefits of using a business account rather than a personal or creator account. But there are a few more factors that we haven't discussed yet. If we compare the three account types, here are some features a business account will offer:

➤ Schedule and Auto Publish.

➤ Book appointments.

➤ Promote branded content.

➤ Insights and analytics.

➤ Additional contact options.

➤ 2-Tab inbox.

➤ Check branded content insights on Facebook.

➤ Create and manage ads.

➤ Promote posts.

Booking Feature

A less discussed and used feature offered by Instagram's business account is the booking feature. With the provision of your location and website, all your followers can visit your office or physical location, but they can also book an appointment. Instagram has tied up with a lot of scheduling and appointment-tracking software such as MyTime, Shore, Appointments by Square, Acuity Scheduling, and StyleSeat, among many others. You can also find a "Reserve" feature for restaurants and cafes or ticket selling options for popular concerts and shows.

To recap, here's how you'll use your business profile to promote your brand. Create a profile, revamp it with a suitable display picture and an appealing bio, think of a creative theme and a username, create content, post and promote it, find relevant users to follow, and use tactics to create maximum interaction. The CTA (call to action) buttons like the website link and contact details, along with the analytics and demographics, are additional helpful features.

After so much discussion on setting up a business profile, we're sure that yours is going to stand out from others. Now, it's time to delve further into practical Instagram marketing. We will start with content creation and the importance of staying consistent with it.

PART 2: PRACTICAL INSTAGRAM MARKETING

Chapter 5: Creating Consistent Content (That Converts)

The first chapter on practical Instagram marketing will focus on one of the most important aspects of social media: content. Content can either define your brand or completely ruin its image. A sure-fire way of winning Instagram is posting quality content and with consistency. And by consistency, we mean posting at least once a day. Instagram's algorithm works in a way that supports and pushes forward content that is posted consistently, hence giving you easy recognition, more followers, and in turn, more sales. Being consistent is one thing, but producing quality content is another. Both should go hand-in-hand.

Here are some intriguing ways through which you can create quality content and keep it consistent with reaching your goals:

Optimizing for Your Small Business Profile

Since we've already talked about setting up a business profile and optimizing it for a small business, we won't go into much detail on it again. We've just mentioned it here due to its important role in boosting content and turning it into leads and sales. To recap briefly, your username, profile picture, and bio must be utterly compelling, with effective call to action buttons such as a working link to your website and contact details like a phone number or physical location. An important factor that'll lure your followers into staying on your profile and visiting it often is your content.

Taking Quality Pictures

High-quality images are extremely important on social media, and to achieve those, we'd suggest you go through these helpful tips:

Arrange an Appropriate Setup

Professional equipment like a good camera, video recorder, and a laptop are the most basic tools required for taking high-quality pictures. Even though phone cameras are pretty good nowadays, investing in a professional camera will give your photographs the professional edge they deserve. If you don't have the necessary photography skills, we'd recommend learning them to use them for a long time until you can afford a professional freelancer—but more about that later in this chapter.

To take amazing pictures, you'll need an appropriate setup. You need to learn a few basic rules about the setup, such as incorporating natural light, exposure of the image, or capturing a picture at the golden hour. The composition is also important. The textures, shapes, and colors of the subject form the "rule of thirds" that balance the image within the invisible grid for proper composition. Consider your viewpoint and frame of the subject to capture images in the best possible way.

Use Third-Party Apps and Tools

You can use a lot of third-party apps to either edit your images or use readily available photos to manipulate them according to your preferences. A lot of editing apps and software such as VSCO, Aviary, Layout, Adobe Lightroom, Snapseed, Afterlight, and many more are available out there to add soul to your photos. Additional tools such as Adobe Stock, iStock, or Piktochart help in providing professionally shot photographs or tools to create infographics and presentations for your company.

A Few Ideas to Shoot Creative Pictures

Here are a few examples of how different natural elements or concepts can be used to your benefit:

- **Minimalism**

Minimal content is serving the millennials and younger generation with a sense of satisfaction and simplicity. Minimalism has been all the rage lately, with people trying to incorporate as few elements as possible in their picture frames. This approach is aesthetically appealing and grabs the attention of users.

- **Colors and Patterns**

A colorful Instagram feed is always appealing. When you're choosing a color palette before finalizing the aesthetic theme of your brand, you need to keep in mind the type of content you're going to present to your target audience. Sticking to that color palette and aesthetic theme, you can choose subjects that offer a different pop of color to create contrast and patterns that portray certain textures to add liveliness to the frame.

- **Backgrounds and Details**

These two aspects are the most captivating shots within images. Whether it's textured wallpaper or a farm full of colorful flowers, any background that stands out can be used as an appealing backdrop to capture your subject. Similarly, shots of details can also provide your feed with a different look. These are fresh, calm, and professional.

Posting Your Pictures

How to Post Pictures

Once your images are ready, you can start posting them using your business profile. Here's a step-by-step guide on how to do this:

➢ Make sure that you have downloaded all the required images in your phone gallery.

After clicking on the plus (+) sign at the bottom-center of the app, you'll be given a window to click on images or record a video.

➢ Since you have the images in your gallery, tap on the "Choose from Gallery" option.

➢ You can then adjust the size of the image, crop it, or select multiple images if required, for what's known as a "carousel" post. If you download an associated app called "Layout" it also lets you form collages.

➢ Edit the image(s) using the provided filters or manual editing tools such as brightness, contrast, vignette, or sharpness.

➢ Click "Next" when you're satisfied with the filter and type a relevant caption along with the required hashtags.

➢ Finally, add the location, tag people, or other accounts in the image, and determine whether you want to share it to Facebook or not.

Creating Consistent Content

To understand this point better, we're going to consider an example or situation where you're starting a fashion styling company or a garments business. This would help you gain thorough insight and get a better understanding of how to create consistent content. These steps are useful in creating content that will last for at least a week or a month, depending on the amount you shoot in a day. There are many more ways to stay consistent, but in our opinion, this seems to work the best. You'll always have something to post, and it will be quality content.

Step 1: Select the Type of Content and Create an Inspiration Board

Your fashion company will require a lot of photoshoots with models and your brand's garments. This would be your basic content type. To create an edge, you can shoot videos of the backstage or behind the scenes. You could also hire influencers who are into micro-blogging and hand over your social media handle to them for a day.

Once you select and plan out the content you want to put up for the week or the following month, you need to create an inspiration board. It basically works like a Pinterest board that gives you plausible ideas for content generation. It'll also make your content strategies clearer.

Step 2: Create a Brief or a Detailed Plan

This is when you schedule the entire plan along with all locations and respective timings for the photoshoot. Once you know your content type and style, it's time to create a plan accordingly. You'll need to coordinate this with the models if you're hiring any. Keeping a plan handy will map out your entire day's schedule, making it easier for you to move and shoot. This will also help to save time and money.

Step 3: Hire a Photographer, a Freelancer, or Learn the Skill Yourself

If you're a business owner who's just starting out, you'll probably be on a budget. But if you can manage the funding, we'd recommend hiring a professional photographer or a freelancer to carry out the shoot for your website and social media content. If not, learn to photograph subjects using online tutorials or a basic course to save money every time you want to conduct a shoot. Good photography is important when it comes to presenting your products to your audience, and it shows the professional and serious side of your business.

Step 4: Put the Plan in Action

Once you've got the photography tools ready to create content, and devised a plan, put it into action. Try to stay ahead of schedule in order not to be overwhelmed with any obstacles. It's an important day for you as you're shooting to gather a major chunk of content, so be prepared accordingly. When you're done with it, get to editing and preparing your final posts and content for your website and social media at the earliest. Schedule them when you're all done, and you're ready with almost a month's worth of content.

Chalene Johnson's Expert Content Engagement Tips

Chalene Johnson is one of the top social media marketers out there and a popular business podcast speaker. A social-media-savvy entrepreneur, she has some of the best tips to engage the audience on social media with your brand.

Tip 1: Interact with Your Audience

The first and foremost step in creating engagement with your audience is to interact with them. If you create posts that ask questions or demand followers to tag their friends, you'll fetch a steady interaction in your comments section. Try replying to their comments to make your followers feel that they are heard. It increases the value of your brand and establishes trust. Stories are a great way to increase interaction; you can put up polls and quizzes, hold questions and answers, or use story templates. If you manage to create a good amount of interaction on comments and threads, you've succeeded. It's even better if you're receiving personal messages through DMs. That's when you know you've truly succeeded.

Tip 2: Keep Your Content Edgy and Different

Instagram is saturated with a common kind of content now. You can see everyone posting Pinterest-ready images or videos of their products. You need to create content that is edgy and different to stand out from other brands. Users are bored of seeing monotonous content and expect something new every now and then. You need to keep your content different from others and create something that your users can relate to. It can be something personal or heartfelt, for example:

- Sharing Experience Through Content

Brands like GoPro sponsor customers through trips; sharing users' thrilling experiences on its Instagram page. This provides its followers with fresh visual content and creates more engagement.

- Behind-the-Scenes Content

As we've already explained before and will discuss further in the upcoming chapters, behind-the-scenes content has been—and still is—a major game-changer in establishing trust between brands and followers.

- Content That Appeals to Emotions

Levi's Philippines recently created an ad that featured a father customizing a jacket for his blind son in Braille. It was not only successful in winning the Outstanding Marketing Award at the biggest national retail awards show but was also appreciated by the global audience. This really helped Levi's to gain more followers and generate more sales. You can follow a similar pattern and generate content that is heartfelt.

Tip 3: Pay Attention to New Features

Whenever Instagram introduces a new feature, it attracts a lot of attention. Many marketing agencies underestimate this aspect and tend to ignore the new features until they're overused. Chalene Johnson suggests working with Instagram and being updated about new features at every step. For instance, when the feature of IGTV was rolled out, not many marketers paid attention to it. IGTV videos slowly gained traction and have now become a major factor in almost all marketing strategies. Instagram has realized this potential and is planning to put a lot of money and thought into this feature to develop it further.

Chalene Johnson ran a test in which she posted an IGTV video without the preview button, and then a similar IGTV video the next week with the preview button. She noticed that the former video got only 3,000 views compared to 60,000 views in the second video. This shows that we need to use what Instagram is presenting us and listen to what the app has to say.

Tip 4: Don't Just Create Content, Promote It

It's absolutely useless to create content and sit back, hoping the world will see it. Even if you create flawless content that's out of this world, what's the point if there aren't many people to consume it? You need to create plans and strategies to promote your content and get it out there. Whether you need to make it aesthetically appealing or informative, your customers should save your posts for whatever reason.

But don't overdo it. Chalene Johnson claims that watching the same content through cross-promotions and seeing it up on stories time and again bores and frustrates the audience. A lot of brands use only stories to promote their content. Even though a lot of users prefer watching stories to other types of content, promoting your posts every day on stories is ineffective. No one likes to see the multiple small dots that make up ten to fifteen stories for a particular brand. If you want your followers to read a specific piece of text, you can record a short video and incorporate the text into it, instead of keeping the text itself on for six seconds, which will be hardly readable, or repeating it within multiple stories.

As we all know, consistency is the key. Use all the available resources and educate yourself on how to create the best quality content consistently. This is the main factor that'll determine the success of your brand on this social media platform. Define your goals, prepare strategies for your content, and stick to the plan.

Chapter 6: How to Use Hashtags to Attract Customers

Before delving into how the hashtags help in attracting customers and clients, let's first talk about how this massive internet phenomenon came into existence.

History of the Hashtag

It all started with a simple tweet by Chris Messina, a designer, speaker, and an avid Twitter user. His tweet dated 23rd August 2007 read, "How do you feel about using # (pound) for groups. As in #barcamp [msg]?"

The idea behind this tweet, as he explains, was to introduce, to some extent, contextualization, content filtering, and exploratory serendipity within Twitter. Little did he know that in a short span of time, the concept of the hashtag would receive wide acceptance across different social media platforms and become a frequently used metadata tag. While he was inspired by a similar use of "#" on other sites, he is widely credited as the inventor of the hashtag as we know it today.

It may have originated on Twitter, but the concept of hashtags and its potential in grouping similar posts is extremely relevant to any social media platform that deals with quick and dynamic content. So, it wasn't exactly a surprise that Instagram, with its vibrant visual content, took the hashtags to a whole new level.

A simple explanation of a "hashtag" is a keyword or phrase that is prefixed by the "#" symbol, whose objective is to group user-generated content of the same type or theme.

While the advantages and convenience of hashtags are proved beyond any doubt now, initially, people hated them mainly because of how they looked on their timelines. But, before they knew it, hashtags were adopted so widely that nearly 24% of measured tweets contain hashtags now.

A Glance at Hashtags on Instagram

Instagram adopted hashtags even better than Twitter. A staggering 66.6% of Instagram posts contain hashtags. That's two-thirds of all the content that's generated on Instagram! With hashtags being used so extensively, they obviously have marketing potential if used smartly and appropriately. We will see how in the upcoming sections.

According to Mention's *Instagram Engagement Report 2018,* which is based on data from 115 million Instagram posts, the five most commonly used hashtags were #love, #instagood, #fashion, #photooftheday, and #style. However, they were not the most useful tags. That credit goes to the ones that actually manage to boast the highest average engagement rate. Those are #ad, #comedy, and #meme. The #ad, as the name suggests, is used to denote sponsored content, which highlights the power of influencer marketing on this platform.

Other statistics suggest that an Instagram post with at least one hashtag enjoys 12.6% more engagement than a post without any hashtags. This clearly indicates that if you are planning on growing your Instagram account's marketing potential, it is imperative to be on top of your hashtag game.

Why Hashtags Are Important on Instagram

Over the past decade, Instagram, as an app, has undergone several changes. However, throughout the process, the hashtags held their ground. The reason is simple—they are too important to do away with!

Using the right kind of hashtags, targeting a specific audience on posts and stories is still one of the best strategies to achieve a consistent flow of fresh audiences to your Instagram account. The smart use of hashtags has immense potential to improve your engagement rate and the number of your followers, which directly translates into more business for your brand.

A public Instagram account with posts carrying a relevant hashtag will be displayed on that particular hashtag's page. Some users follow the hashtag pages to consume relevant content rather than following the Instagram accounts. This audience base does form a significant source of the traffic to your posts. This is a great way to reach the target audience with whom you had no prior engagement. If you can impress the first-timers with quality and relevant content, they are surely going to be your followers.

For all practical purposes, hashtags on Instagram can be described as keywords with which you can maximize the visibility of your posts. You simply can't imagine building an attractive and highly successful Instagram account without taking complete advantage of hashtags' marketing potential.

Things to Remember Before Devising Your Own Hashtags

First of all, if your Instagram profile is private, the hashtags associated with your posts will not be displayed in the respective hashtag pages. If attracting more customers/clients is your primary objective, then a private profile seriously restricts your chances. Of course, once you gain the required level of popularity, you can afford to go private to exercise control over the type of followers that consume your content. But for beginners, a public account offers much better growth potential.

The structure of hashtags allows for the use of numbers, but blank spaces and special characters are not permitted. Also, you can use hashtags only on your own content and cannot use them to tag posts from other users.

While the overuse of hashtags on a single post may not fetch you the required results—using too many hashtags dilutes the specificity of your content—Instagram permits you to use up to 30 hashtags on posts and up to 10 hashtags on stories.

Types of Instagram Hashtags and Their Advantages

There are different types of hashtags in use on Instagram, and understanding them is vital to coming up with an efficient hashtag strategy for your account. The three main categories are community hashtags, branded hashtags, and campaign hashtags.

Community Hashtags

As the name indicates, community hashtags are designed to bring together like-minded people. It is a great way to establish your own community and gain followers with similar tastes and inclinations. Community hashtags also improve the searchability of your posts.

There are several sub-types of community hashtags that indicate your products or services (e.g., #coffeeshop, #pizza, etc.), hashtags that indicate your professional niche (e.g., #eventplanner, #DJ), hashtags for Instagram communities in your niche (e.g., #carspottersofinstagram, #foodiesofinstagram), hashtags for special events or seasons (e.g., #independenceday, #internationalgirlchildday), location-specific hashtags (e.g., #madeinIndia, #detroitmachines, #italiancuisine), daily hashtags (e.g., #throwbackthursday, #mondaymotivation, #wheeliewednesday), hashtags containing phrases related to your activities (e.g., #carlove, #drivefastdrivesafe), hashtags for acronyms (e.g., #motd—meme of the day), and hashtags with emojis (while special characters aren't allowed, you can certainly employ emojis as hashtags.)

Using a variety of community hashtags on your posts can help you reach different yet relevant communities. For example, if you own a custom car garage in Detroit, you can use the hashtag #customcarbuilderindetroit to cover potential customers looking for a mod-job, and you can also use #lifeofcustomcarbuilder to attract enthusiasts who are interested in your daily life as a car modifier.

Branded Hashtags

Branded hashtags are a great way to develop your brand identity and coverage on Instagram. The hashtag can be your company name, product name, or even tagline. It can also be a strong indicator of your brand identity rather than being your brand name itself. For example, Nike's #justdoit works very well as a brand hashtag. The sportswear brand manages to make its followers use its hashtag, which is a great way to spread the reach and lure in a new audience.

Another advantage of using branded hashtags is that you can keep a tab on the hashtag page to gain insight into where and in which context your followers are using your business's tag. This can be helpful in tweaking your hashtag strategy or even floating an effective marketing campaign.

Campaign Hashtags

Campaign hashtags differ from the previous two types in the duration of use. While the community and branded tags are meant to last forever, campaign hashtags are seasonal or even run for just a few days. If your business or page needs a shot in the arm, campaign hashtags are the way to go.

Needless to say, campaign hashtags are usually associated with new product launches, limited period offers, a temporary partnership, etc. All of these activities can reach their maximum potential with the right usage of campaign hashtags.

Finding the Best Hashtags for Your Instagram Account

While it may be tempting and intuitive to use the most commonly used hashtags like #love and #instagood on your posts, you should know that these tags that are used millions of times don't really work well to bring you a new audience. They relegate your interesting post to a needle in a haystack, reducing its potential to reach your target audience.

The more niche your hashtag is, the better the engagement rate on your post. For example, if you own an Instagram account to promote your custom car-building business, instead of using a generic and common hashtag like #carsofinstagram or #vintagecar, you could use more specific hashtags like #americancustom, #customfordmustang, and so on.

At the end of the day, finding the best hashtags for your account makes all the difference in determining whether you reach the target audience and grow your following or not. There are a few proven ways to find the tags that best suit your business and page.

Know Your Audience's Pulse

Coming up with hashtags spontaneously is not going to help you reach the right target audience. It is imperative for you to select your target audience and analyze their behavior, the type of hashtags they use, and pick the ones that are suitable for your page, products, and services. By doing so, you will discover hashtags that are not only relevant but also double up as keywords that people on Instagram are actually searching for.

Check Out What Your Competitors Are Doing

Competitive intelligence is important in any type of business, and setting up a successful Instagram account is no different. Knowing what type of hashtags your competitors prefer will give you reliable insight into the tags that tend to generate engagement. While you may not need to compete with your rival's hashtags, exploring them will give you an idea of what makes your target audience tick. More often than not, you will end up finding a unique hashtag that goes well with your page.

See What Industry Leaders Are Doing

The top Instagram influencers in your field or the ones who have similar target audiences are on the top because they must be doing things right. So, it is always a good idea to monitor them closely to uncover some high-quality hashtags for your own use. You can learn a lot more from the top influencers in your niche than just discovering new hashtags. Their content could inspire you or even give you new and interesting ideas.

Explore Closely Related Tags

If you're enjoying success with a hashtag, it always pays to monitor posts from others with the same hashtag and search for other tags that are associated with it. Often, this exercise will lead you to other highly successful hashtags that are closely related to your crowd-puller. If you find such related tags, use them to amplify your reach.

Ways to Optimize Your Instagram Hashtags

Like any other search-based channel, Instagram's hashtag strategy should evolve with the platform's ever-changing algorithms and best practices. An excellent hashtag strategy reaches not only a maximum number of people but also the right kind of people for your business. That's where optimizing your hashtags comes into play.

The best way to optimize and fine-tune your hashtag strategy is to monitor the analytics closely to measure the performance of your past hashtags. This will help you increase the number of hashtags that work for your page and business. Instagram's analytics tool, Insights, tells you how many people landed on your page via the hashtags you used. Alternatively, you can use one of the many paid third-party analytics apps like Later, which offers even more insights like which hashtags are driving more likes, comments, saves, impressions, and reach. These services also give you objective information regarding the performance of your new hashtags.

The best way to maximize the potential of a hashtag is to try and get into the coveted "Top Posts" category for that hashtag. This naturally directs a lot of traffic your way. For a post to get into the top list, you need to ensure that it gets a high level of engagement in a relatively short period of time. Basically, it needs to be interesting and viral. This tells Instagram's algorithm that your post is of top quality and highly entertaining.

You can also add your clickable branded hashtags on your Instagram bio so that they can convert into website visits. Also, don't miss the opportunity to add hashtags to your stories. You can do this either by using the text box feature (this lets you add up to 10 tags) or by using a hashtag tool to come up with the most relevant hashtag.

One of the most important Instagram updates in 2018 was the feature that allows users to follow hashtags. This is a great opportunity for businesses to maximize engagement with their audiences. If you can get your followers also to follow your unique branded hashtags, then your posts can appear twice on their timeline—once because they follow your page and once again because they follow your hashtag.

Running hashtag-based campaigns and competitions is another popular way to empower your hashtag and optimize its potential.

How Many Hashtags to Use per Post?

Well, there is no straightforward answer to this question. While some experts recommend that you use as many hashtags as possible to maximize your reach, some believe that sticking to five per post produces the best possible results and keeps things within the target audience. The bottom line is, it all depends on your niche, the nature of your posts, and the width of your target audience base. It is advisable to mix it up until you find the right balance for your unique Instagram account.

Hashtags are the superstars of Instagram. By now, you must have realized the immense positive impact a properly calibrated hashtag strategy can have on customers or clients. It helps you build a long-lasting relationship with your followers, as well. So, we recommend that you keep these points in mind while devising your own unique hashtag strategy.

Chapter 7: Stories: 6 Ways to Build Your Brand

We all have to agree to the fact that there's something about stories that drives curiosity and excitement. It's amazing to see how brands and users try to squeeze in every drop of creativity within their content to stand out. Stories are a great tool for such brands. Among the one billion active users on Instagram to date, around half of them—500 million users, that is—watch stories on a daily basis. Since the advent of stories, people have had more content to watch on Instagram. Not only are they using this app more and staying on it for longer, but they are also dedicating 50% of their time viewing stories instead of posts; so much so that influencers and marketers are publishing fewer feed posts and more stories since 2016, which is when stories came into the picture. Feed posts are predicted to decline even further this year.

If you're already intrigued, that's great, because we're going to discuss everything about stories in this chapter. This includes what they are, why they are popular, why you should use them for marketing your business, and how to use them.

Why Use Stories for Business Marketing?

Initially designed as a means of simple interaction or sharing small glimpses of life, stories were the epitome of light content that users enjoyed watching. Slowly but steadily, businesses and brands started to realize the potential of this niche and used it to market their content. Unsurprisingly, these caught on among users, and the marketing strategies of businesses took off. But what is the secret behind these stories, and why have they become so popular?

The concept of stories was initially invented by Snapchat. Then, it was steadily adopted by Facebook and Instagram as one of their main features. Stories are basically light content that disappears within 24 hours. They are raw and fresh, and they appeal to users because of their essence. These are also extremely powerful to convey information and relevant data. Compelling stories are a great way to enhance the understanding and receptivity between two sources.

Stories are basically designed to be vertically-formatted and take up the entire phone screen. It's interesting to watch content that fits in the whole window. Users no longer have to rotate their phones, squint their eyes, or zoom in to watch content. It's fast, easy, and convenient. It's also a boon to companies as they don't need to stress on producing fresh content for their stories every few months. Followers might not entirely recall all content that a particular brand produces. They might, however, remember the impact or impression that the content had on them. Brands can always tweak or twist old content to present it in a fresh way.

Also, stories aren't necessarily direct ads that could otherwise be off-putting for followers. They often don't have any direct intention to sell products or convince customers to buy any brand's services. We're not talking about story ads here. Businesses and marketing agencies are putting a lot of effort into producing story content that stands out. To know what already works and what will work this year, we've curated a list with some tips of how to use them for marketing your business.

But before that, let's talk about how to create a simple story.

How to Create Stories

Creating stories isn't rocket science, obviously. Follow these simple steps, and you'll be good to go.

Step 1: Capturing Content

Open the Instagram app, and you'll notice a camera icon on the top-left corner. Tap on it, and the window will direct you to the camera function to record your content. A big circle placed on the bottom center of the window is used to either shoot an image or record a video by holding it down to film. You can also upload an image or video from your phone gallery by accessing the tiny thumbnail on the bottom-left corner.

Step 2: Adding Features

When you have shot or decided what content to upload, you need to set the viewing frame. This is what your followers will see when they tap on your story. You can either leave it to cover the entire screen or pinch the image and zoom it in or out. Next, you can add various features such as text, location, and temperature by using the third icon on the top. To enhance it, you can add fun features such as stickers, GIFs, or even mentions and tags.

Step 3: Uploading It

After preparing the frame and adding all the required features, press the "Add to Story" button. You can decide whether to hide it from someone or form a closed group to share it with only chosen followers. You can also add the snaps or videos to your highlight panel.

After you're done, you can check the number of followers that viewed your story by clicking on it once it has been uploaded.

6 Ways to Use Stories for Your Brand

1. Boomerang and Hyperlapse

Boomerang and Hyperlapse are fun ways to create engagement with your stories. Boomerangs are short videos or GIFs that create a back-and-forth loop of the captured moments. They are majorly used by the younger generation, mostly within stories. Hyperlapse is another creative feature that captures short time-lapse videos. The app uses your smartphone's accelerometer to capture smooth videos and create a hyperlapse. These two tactics are useful in creating digestible content that is truly engaging.

2. Contests or Giveaways

As we've previously mentioned, contests and giveaways are the best way to create major engagement and encourage people to follow your brand. A lot of businesses realize the importance of giving away free items to generate sales and revenue. How this works is that you announce contests to win free trips or your newly launched products by requesting your followers to follow and subscribe to your page, and share it with a number of other friends. This helps you gain more followers and basically a lot of potential customers. Contests and giveaways have gained a lot of traction lately, and we'd highly recommend using this tactic to lure more customers.

3. Converting Your Blog into Stories

A lot of brands run blogs on their websites that contain information about their products or their discipline. Even though they may have excellent content, visibility decreases due to the saturation in the market. To overcome this issue, you can use the feature of stories to drive more traffic to your blog. At times, you just want to make your customers aware of the information that your blog provides, which can be reflected in your stories in bits and pieces. You can plan a bunch of stories on a particular day during the week and assign a blog post to each, using creative infographics and a link to the post. This leads to improved brand awareness and more traffic to your blog or website.

4. Polls or Q&As

Poll stickers and emoji slider stickers are the new way to create engagement with your audience. These are used to ask questions to customers or demand their opinions. Polls include two options that need to be answered by the story viewer. Users can also react to stories by voicing their opinion on any question by sliding the emoji. It shows the reaction percentage by other users. Poll questions like "Which product do you prefer out of the two?" or "Which outfit would you prefer?" can easily compel your audience to answer. You can also use the feature of conducting quizzes or a set of Q&As by presenting a question and giving four options with a correct answer among A, B, C, and D. A great example of a brand that constantly uses polls and emoji sliders is Lush Cosmetics. The brand has figured out its way of creating powerful interaction with their customers, which helps in driving more sales.

5. Adding Links to Stories

After reaching 10,000 followers, Instagram gives you the option of adding links to your stories. This solves a huge problem: the inability to add clickable links to your posts. Whether it's your blog article, newly launched products, or an update to your mobile application, you can add the link to your story after sharing relevant information on it. This grabs the attention of your followers and evokes curiosity in them. An amazing aspect of this feature is that users don't need to leave the Instagram interface; instead, the link directly opens within the app, making it completely convenient for them. It also increases footfall and traffic on your website, helping to significantly increase sales.

6. Story Highlights

Even though stories are disappearing content that lasts only up to 24 hours, you can permanently keep them on your feed by adding them to your highlights. There's an option called "Add to Highlight" at the bottom of the story. You can create a highlight panel with a title that'll act as an album of your favorite or important stories. There's no limitation to the number of highlights panels or the number of stories in each album. It's an amazing way to keep your important brand moments highlighted on your feed. This is specifically useful when you've covered important events during your journey and want to keep them visible throughout.

Ways to Drive More Traffic

Keep Your Stories Short and Sweet

As we discussed above, no one likes a parade of stories that are repetitive and monotonous. In such cases, the majority of users fail to pay attention to your content, even if it is credible. Stick to a maximum of ten stories to tell your tale. Anything above that is bound to have fewer views than anticipated. You need to stick to the point and avoid multiple stories, especially if there's no connection between them. A great tactic to keep your story on the front row is to schedule and post stories after a while, say three to four hours. This lets your viewers find you easily, and you can have more views on your latest stories.

Use IGTV with Stories

While we've talked about IGTV stories multiple times, we're mentioning them again due to the importance they hold—and we will be mentioning them further in the following chapters, too. But here, we're going to talk about integrating IGTV videos with your stories. You can post a link leading to the full-length IGTV video on your story, and add the relevant link to the IGTV description. We already know that you cannot add clickable links on posts, so this feature is extremely helpful.

Create a Story—Have a Beginning and an End

Stories are called this for a reason. They demand that you tell a story that's alluring, captivating, and interesting. You have a blank canvas to produce short, creative anecdotes that can create a lasting impression on your followers. While you're storyboarding your content, try to have an interesting beginning and a satisfying end, with content that resonates with the viewers. Even if you're posting stories during no fixed hours that are spread throughout the day, you need to make sure that all stories connect. Make sure that they have a good flow. End the stories with greetings or a simple "Thank you" to your viewers.

Create Your Own Style

When you put effort into your content, it shows. Many people take stories lightly and aren't willing to put much effort into story content as it disappears within 24 hours. They don't realize that stories are watched more than posts and leave a great impression of your brand. That's why it's important to create your own style that reflects your brand identity. Pick certain fonts, a color palette, or a theme that looks distinguished and marks your brand's recognition. It shouldn't be monotonous, either. Play with your content, but keep a subtle trait of your brand to make it stand out.

Using Instagram stories for marketing in 2020 is a great step toward reaching your goals. However, it should be noted that these tactics and strategies shouldn't be repetitive and frequent. That's why it is important to build a marketing strategy and content plan that'll instruct you on the type of content to be used beforehand.

Chapter 8: Using Video to Drive Traffic

Now that we've explored images and story content let's move on to another engaging content type, which is video. Video content has lately been a powerful marketing tool, and will further grow this year, as well. Around 80% of people online watch videos for entertainment and information over other content types. You can benefit from this by including video content in your marketing planning. Realizing this, 63% of marketing agencies have already incorporated video marketing into their strategies and content plan.

This is why, in this chapter, we will focus on all the "whys" and "hows" regarding video content.

Benefits of Using Video Content for Small Businesses

Helps in Turning Views to Leads

Among all content, video content has the highest rate of conversion. Around 71% of marketers have claimed that video marketing is more successful than other content forms and that it gives the highest leads. The majority of followers who watch a video are compelled to share it on their stories or through direct messages. This leads to more followers and traffic on your website, ultimately leading to higher sales. Among them, around 74% of visitors tend to buy a product, hence generating revenue. You just need to pay more attention to your content matter, and the rest will follow on its own. Simply put, a view is generally converted into a successful lead.

People Pay More Attention

Compared to other content types, users are bound to pay more attention to video content as it holds the ability to evoke feelings and emotions. It's a great way to build relationships with your followers. It also shows the hard work and effort put behind the campaigns. As discussed, video content that has something relevant or informative gets more attention. For instance, 90% of viewers claim that they learn about new products and their functioning through videos rather than text. This also applies to entertaining and descriptive videos.

More Social Shares

According to statistics, around 76% of viewers claim to share an entertaining video with their friends, even if it belongs to a brand. With the business tools of Instagram, you can view the number of shares of every video and determine the content type that works. Anything that's relatable, personalized, humorous, or creative is bound to be shared more. Hence, it's important to stand out and create something different. A great example of this is animated videos. They are simple, entertaining, and informative at the same time. You can create pitches with freelancers and post animated content every once in a while.

Extremely Descriptive

Not only is video content easy to consume and digest; it is also a fun way to learn. Most content creators try to pack in as much information as they can in a short video of around 10 to 15 minutes. Punchy videos that are even shorter than that are also a very effective way to get new viewers to engage. A few minutes is an appropriate time frame to grab your followers' attention. As mentioned before, most of the users prefer learning about a product or subject through a video rather than reading. That's one of the reasons why marketers prefer to make videos. It's also great for all lazy buyers who'd otherwise refrain from online shopping due to long product descriptions. Videos make it easy for them to make quick decisions and hence help you sell more products.

Good Return on Investment

Not only is video content engaging and interactive, but it's also a great source of ROI for time and money. You can imagine the time, effort, and money required to prepare a video. It's also difficult at times. We talked about the equipment and tools required to shoot a video, and these aren't cheap. So, they add to the cost, and you sometimes have to go beyond the budget. However, since a lot of users engage in video content and are directed to your website, it is highly likely that they'll end up buying a product. This drives more sales and helps in reaching your target. It makes it worth all the money, time, and effort invested.

The Necessary Equipment to Shoot a Video

If you already have the skill set to shoot videos, you just need a smartphone with a good camera to do the job. But a few companies prefer to go the extra mile and use professional tools such as a video recorder or a high-quality DSLR camera. Apart from that, you'll just need a few lenses and a fixed yet appealing backdrop to shoot all your videos, except for when you need a change in your content. A tripod stand and portable studio lights are additional tools to enhance your videos and still photos. You might also need a few third-party tools to edit your videos.

Shooting an Instagram Video

Whether it's a 15-second video to post on your feed or a 10-minute, vertically-formatted IGTV video, we've got you covered with some of the best tips on recording your video content. Now, there are two ways of doing this. You can either casually shoot a video of your surroundings by opening the app and clicking on the center button to start recording, or shoot a professional video using proper equipment, then upload it on your profile. Either way, just follow these steps:

Step 1: Consider the Aspect Ratio

Whether it's shooting for your feed or for your IGTV video, the format is vertical. Considering this, the aspect ratio needs to be 9:16, which is also the perpendicular position of normal videos; so you need to adjust your camera accordingly. Even though Instagram allows you to upload landscape-oriented content now, we'd recommend shooting and uploading vertical content as it is more convenient to watch, thus more commonly preferred.

Step 2: Set Your Camera

If you're using a smartphone to shoot, you're already good with the aspect ratio. You'll just need a phone stand. With a DSLR, you need to flip the camera to a 90° position. Set the tool on a tripod stand and adjust your subject's position.

• Pro-Tip

A tripod ball head can assist you in accurately shooting a 9:16 aspect ratio with a DSLR camera. Fix the ball head to a tripod plate, attach it to your tripod, and fix the camera to the ball head. You can adjust, tilt, or pan the camera according to your preference to have a smooth and proportionate shot. You can also use a camera stabilizer, monopod, studio lights, or a slider to have professional results.

You might also need a microphone in case you want to add a conversation or sound in your video. A small mic is often attached to the shirt or blouse of the person who is speaking in the video. This allows for clear audio and adds a professional touch to it.

Step 3: Shoot and Edit

As soon as you have your equipment and setup ready, it's time to shoot. Take multiple shots and video samples of the chosen subject, according to your storyboard. Tap on the camera screen on the point where you want to keep focus.

To edit your video, you can choose from the row of filters available on the app if you've shot on your phone. You can also use some of the amazing third-party apps to edit your videos with special effects, and to delete unnecessary shots.

To choose music for your video, you can use some of the external tools and useful apps such as SoundCloud, AudioJungle, or Soundstripe. Other useful apps to help you cut frames, change the orientation, and edit the video overall are VideoCrop, InShot, and CutStory, among others.

And that's it! You're ready to upload your video.

Types of Video Content to Create Engagement

Humor and Light Content

Humor is our favorite way of creating engagement! We suggest that you incorporate it into your video content to garner a lot of attention. Preparing content that is light, funny, and catchy is imperative. You can find a lot of young people sharing memes and sarcastic posts all over Instagram. Dive into puns and current affairs, or mix trending memes with your content to give your followers a light chuckle. Using parody in any popular subject can also grab a few eyeballs. This shows the clever side of your team, and needless to say, the younger generation highly appreciates wit and comedy.

Interviews with Team Members or Clients

While you're planning your content strategies, you can consider an interview shoot with your team members once a month. You can either interview different team members in every video or hold a collective meet-and-greet that includes quizzes, interviews, and games with your entire team. Your audience would like to know the faces behind your awesome brand, and it'd make them trust you more.

Video testimonials with clients are the most honest form of content that you can present to your viewers. If you trust your products and are sure that you'll fetch positive reviews, you can try them out. Since they are true, your potential customers would get an honest opinion and would trust your brand while buying your products.

Live Videos

Live videos have proven to be one of the most engaging content creation techniques so far. They come with a lot of added benefits, too. These are easy to create, take up less time, and need no thorough planning. Live videos let your audience interact with you in real-time, without any filter. Your followers can react to your live videos and share live comments. You can also hold interactive sessions by answering your followers' questions, or by handing over your account to an influencer who belongs to your discipline. This will also help you gather more followers from their accounts.

Personalization

When you tweak the content and personalize it according to your target audience, you're bound to fetch more views. One great example is how Spotify rolled out personalized music statistics according to each user at the end of 2019. A lot of users appreciated this type of content and shared it across various platforms. It helped Spotify to gain a massive number of users in the following time period. You can point out traits or understand your target audience to map out customized content that they'd like and appreciate. Something that's relatable is surely going to be successful among your followers.

DIY or Product Description

If your brand involves selling a product, you definitely need to tap into video marketing. A great way to showcase your products to your customers is by making videos about them. Say, for example, you're managing a makeup brand. There are some great ways to play with your products to create amazing video content. Here are some of those awesome ways to do it:

➢ Motion design or time-lapse video to show the most sought-after or newly launched products.

➢ Collaborating with various influencers who have a strong follower base and hiring them to produce video content showcasing your products.

➤ A DIY or "how to use" video.

➤ Surprising facts about your products or the benefits of using them.

Strategies for Driving More Traffic through Video Content

Use Search Engine Optimization

Whether you're using IGTV videos or short videos that will be posted on your feed and stories, you need to follow other strategies, such as using hashtags, to promote your content. But if you're sharing a glimpse of the main video on your story, you need to provide the website link through which your followers can find the video. In this case, your video also needs to be ranked higher on the Google search list to be seen. This can only be possible with Search Engine Optimization. You need to apply certain keywords and phrases to your video title and description, which will optimize it for better search results. The search engine is designed to search for results according to specific keywords and the common word searches of users.

Prepare Your Content Plan

You need to define your content and decide on its type, depending on your target audience. Since we've discussed a lot of video content ideas, you can choose from the options and prepare a strategic plan accordingly. Every content type that you prefer needs to have a purpose and drive more leads.

The next thing you need to incorporate into your content plan is consistency. We already talked about the importance of being consistent in earlier chapters, so you must know the reason why we're mentioning it again. It'll keep your feed and profile in the top searches, and you're bound to be discovered more easily.

Driving traffic through videos is all about finding that angle that your followers would appreciate and incorporating it into your content. We know it's a big hassle to shoot and upload video content regularly, and that's why we suggest preparing a content plan that works.

Chapter 9: How to Sell Your Products on Instagram

Instagram, being a social media platform with over a billion users, carries immense potential for e-commerce business. As we clearly know by now, it's not just about the size of subscribers. At least 500 million Instagram users log into the platform on a daily basis, and around 640 million users (around 70% of the total subscriber base) follow at least one business account.

Such a vast ocean of potential customers makes Instagram an excellent playground for social media marketers and entrepreneurs alike. As a proactive social media platform, Instagram has been making consistent efforts to make the platform conducive to business and shopping.

The recently introduced Instagram Shopping feature aims to help brands and businesses to generate sales and leads from the platform.

What Is Instagram Shopping?

Available in select markets across North America, in addition to the LATAM, EMEA, and APAC zones, Instagram Shopping is providing brands with a virtual storefront where people can explore products via brands' organic posts and stories. They can also discover your products via "Search" and "Explore" features.

And how does it work? Well, you can use tags or product stickers on your posts and stories, and when the users click them, they take them directly to your product description page that contains images of the product along with a detailed description and the cost. The page also includes a direct link to your website where the users can purchase the product. So, in a nutshell, Instagram Shopping channels potential customers to your product page, giving you a great opportunity to convert the leads into sales.

Basically, it makes it a lot easier for brands to highlight the products that are incorporated into their posts and stories. This feature makes Instagram Shopping an extremely attractive avenue for e-commerce brands.

Before Instagram Shopping came into existence, the customer journey on a branded business's Instagram page used to go like this: the customers would follow your page, enjoy the content, and become interested in the products it offered. They would go on to like and comment on the posts, enquiring about the product, and its availability. Ultimately, they would have to visit the product website to try and search for the product they saw on Instagram. It wasn't guaranteed that every customer who got interested in the product due to the brand's Instagram content would actually put the required effort into finding the product on the website and purchase it. This is an unfavorable situation for both the brand and its prospective clientele.

With the introduction of Instagram Shopping, life has gotten so much easier for both parties. The feature has made moving between two different channels (the social media platform and the seller's website) a seamless process, as a simple click on the Instagram post promoting the product will land the user directly on the page where they can buy it instantly. All the branded page needs to do is tag its products appropriately so that the customers can follow them up easily. Naturally, the conversion rate of prospects into actual customers is much higher with Instagram Shopping.

Now, it's time to answer the obvious question:

How to Sell on Instagram

Well, there are two types of paths you can explore. You can place your products on your posts or your stories. They require different approaches, as we are going to see in the following section.

Selling Products through Posts

➢ First things first. Instagram Shopping is still in the process of being introduced across the world. As of now, the feature is accessible only in select countries, and checking if your country is one of them is the obvious first step.

➢ Once you have determined that Instagram Shopping is indeed active in your country, the next step is to connect your Instagram account to your brand's Facebook channel. That's mandatory!

➢ Once you ensure the cross-connectivity between your Instagram and Facebook channels, you can go about setting up your Instagram business account for your brand. You can convert your personal account into a business account by following a few easy steps. Access your profile's "Settings" and click on "Account." Then, select "Switch to Professional Account." Finally, select "Business" and furnish details regarding the category your business falls into and contact information. Press "Done" and your Instagram business account is good to go. A business profile will give you access to various business features and Instagram Insights, which can be used to gain insights into the engagement rate of your posts and page.

➢ The next step is to set up an Instagram Sales Channel on your Shopify store so that you can add products to your Insta posts and link them to your Shopify store. Before you do this, you need to set up your Facebook page and list your products on the Facebook product catalog (using Facebook Shop).

➢ The above step can be done by logging into your Shopify admin page and clicking the "+" button under the "Sales Channels" heading.

Select "Instagram" under the "Add Sales Channels" dialog and click "Add Channel." Finally, log in to your Facebook account page to authenticate the Instagram account in the sales channel. Once this is done, Instagram will review your account and give you approval. Should you run into a hurdle, you can always raise a ticket with the Instagram help center.

➢ With all the above steps executed, now it's time to take your awesome products to your Instagram followers. You can simply post an image containing your product and tag your products by selecting "Tag Products" button, and click anywhere on your image like you normally do to tag people. Once you click on where you want to place a tag, a search bar will appear, in which you need to type the name of your product exactly as it appears in your store.

Congratulations! You have finally added a post that can enjoy the full benefits of Instagram Shopping. It is to be remembered that there is a limit on the number of products you can tag on an image, so it is useful to have just a limited number of products highlighted per image. If you want to tag more products in a single post, then you can opt for carousel posts (multiple images on a single post).

Selling Products through Instagram Stories

Instagram allows the brand pages to position their products and tag them on the stories so that the users who are interacting with the stories can directly buy products from their favorite brand stores. Given that 300 million Instagram users interact with stories on a daily basis, selling products via stories is too big an opportunity to miss out on.

Moreover, a recent survey by Instagram found that most users interact with a brand page's stories specifically to keep themselves up-to-date with their favorite brand's activities.

Just like selling through Instagram posts, selling through stories is permitted only in select countries where Instagram Shopping is available. You will need an associated Facebook channel, a Shopify account to which you can add an Instagram sales channel, and an Instagram Business Account.

Once all these are set up, you can create stories containing your products, tag them, and lead your customers to the product page on your website. Driving revenue through your Instagram page is a fun way to operate your business while continuing to build an emotional connection with your prospective audience.

Instagram continues to improve its Shopping feature by adding new features to it at regular intervals. The latest additions to Instagram Shopping include a new "Shopping Explore" tab, a "Shop" tab on your business profile, and the functionality of shopping from the videos.

Monitor the Performance of Instagram Shopping

The Instagram Shopping Insights gives you vital analytics that let you measure the success of your product marketing campaign on the social media platform. The analytics include product views (the total number of times the users tapped the product tags and viewed the product page) and "Product" button clicks (the total number of times people clicked on the purchase button on the product page).

Stand out with Creative Content to Enhance Engagement

Like every type of Instagram page, a branded product page needs engagement to be highly successful. Creating outstandingly creative, entertaining content associated with your products is a sure-fire way of bringing in engagement. Also, using hashtags in an efficient way can do wonders when it comes to engagement. This has been discussed in detail earlier in this book.

There is no one way to find success in marketing your products on Instagram. So, you shouldn't be afraid to mix it up and adopt a trial-and-error method to find what works for your business, specific products, and your target audience. Keep experimenting with your product-based content to keep your audience engaged, interested, and wanting to come back for more. Only if you have an adequate amount of traffic to your posts can you set about converting them into your customers.

Keep Abreast of the Evolution of Instagram Shopping

The early adopters of Instagram Shopping have been witnessing huge success. As we mentioned earlier, the social media platform is striving to improve this excellent shopping tool even further to incorporate more features and maximize its potential. So, as the manager of an Instagram Business Account, it is imperative for you to constantly keep tabs on the evolution of the app and the new updates that are coming in.

Explore Upselling and Cross-Selling Tactics

Ask any veteran advertiser, and they will tell you that it is much more expensive to bring a new customer under your brand's umbrella than retaining the existing one. If you also consider the fact that 40% of e-commerce revenue comes from just 8% of its customers, an interesting picture starts to emerge.

So, it is of the utmost importance to devise a strategy to increase your customers' order value and maximize the potential of your business. This is where upselling and cross-selling come into play.

Convincing customers to buy a product from your brand is the hardest part, but once you manage to pull that off, it is much easier to give them a gentle nudge to increase the average order value. It's not very different from a generic consumer entering a supermarket wanting to buy a few specific items but ending up checking out with a shopping cart full of other items. All you need to do is present the other products from your brand—along with the one they are interested in.

- **Cross-Selling**

Now, let's see what cross-selling is. It's a tactic to increase sales by suggesting related or complementary products to the customers. For example, if you manage to convince your customer to buy a pair of shoes, you can create your content in a way that shows how well the shoes go with a pair of socks and pants, and tag those products as well. If the customer is interested in your shoes, the chances are that they will also be interested in buying accessories that go well with them. Cross-selling should be devised in such a way that it'll add value to the customer's initial purchase and improve their overall buying experience.

It is proven that the concept of cross-selling has the potential to improve your revenue by 10 – 30%. This can be easily achieved by making small adjustments to the way you create your Instagram content based on your products.

- **Upselling**

As for upselling, as the name suggests, it is a tactic where you lure the customer into buying a more expensive and fancier product; upgrading the product they were originally interested in; or adding an additional item or items to their order. For example, if you are in the business of selling bikes and the customer entered your product page with interest in an entry-level model, you could alternatively suggest a better one with suspension, disc brakes, a water bottle holder, all-terrain tires, and so on. Usually, if given a choice, a significant number of customers will be happy to buy a superior and better-equipped product. Another example is offering "must have" bike accessories, like a helmet or riding gloves, at the checkout.

Depending on your product portfolio and sales strategy, you can choose to adopt either cross-selling or upselling tactics, or both of them, in order to maximize your revenue.

Now you know the benefits of Instagram Shopping, and how to sell your products on this platform successfully. So, what are you waiting for? It's time to set up your brand page on Instagram and watch your product sales go up. Of course, advertising your business effectively will play a major role in your success, as well. You can find more about that in the next chapter.

Chapter 10: Advertising Your Business through Instagram Ads

If you are advertising your business on digital platforms, but you are still skeptical of Instagram's ability to provide ROI on your advertising budget, this chapter will change your mind. Sure, Instagram may not have as many followers as Facebook, but it is growing at a super-impressive rate, making it a seriously viable platform for advertising your business.

Unlike other digital advertising platforms, text ads are not Instagram's cup of tea. Here, you advertise in the form of images or videos, and this allows you to flex your creative muscles and come up with really impactful and engaging advertising campaigns. Moreover, Instagram allows you to target the right group of people at the right time with apt imagery.

Many advertisers have already started receiving better ROI with Instagram advertising than other channels. With the right strategy and a better understanding of how Instagram works, you, too, can take full advantage of the platform's advertising potential.

How Is Instagram Advertising Different from Other Platforms?

On Instagram, you advertise by paying to post sponsored content to reach the target audience and expand your follower base. The primary objective of this sponsored content is to improve your brand exposure, increase traffic to your business website, generate sales leads, and push the current leads toward conversion.

As we mentioned earlier, the key difference between Instagram ads and those on other social media platforms is that in the former context, text ads are out of the equation. You need images, a set of images, or videos to take your business or products to the target audience.

Let's look at some statistics that firmly underline the importance and effectiveness of advertising on Instagram before delving deeper into the procedure. In March 2017, over 120 million Instagram users visited a website, sought directions, contacted (called, emailed, or direct messaged) to get in touch and know more about a business, based on Instagram ads. According to the social media giant, 60% of Instagrammers say they discovered new products on the platform, and as many as 75% of them take action after being inspired by a post. Any advertiser would admit that these are some seriously impressive numbers.

Instagram Demographics

Before you unload big bucks on Instagram advertising, it would be wise to gain insight into the demographics of Instagram users so as to be sure that your investment is used to reach the right kind of audience for your business.

About 55% of Instagram users belong to the 18 – 29 age brackets, while 28% are 30 – 49 years old. People between the ages of 50 – 64 constitute only 11% of the Instagram population, while only 4% are 65 years or older. So, if your business caters to senior citizens, you would probably be better off taking your advertising investment elsewhere.

However, if your brand deals with products or services that are suitable for the younger age groups, then Instagram Advertising would be an excellent way to reach out to your target audience.

As for geographic segmentation, about 32% of Instagram users live in urban areas, 28% live in the suburbs, and 18% live in the countryside. Women outnumber men on this platform, but the gender gap is steadily diminishing.

Instagram, like most other social media platforms, offers advertisers complete control over their target audiences—like gender, age groups, locations, behaviors, and interests. The app takes advantage of Facebook's massive and well-established demographic data to direct your ads to relevant audiences. This makes Instagram advertising a very powerful tool for advertisers who are looking to target specific niches to prospective customers.

Cost of Instagram Ads

Determining the pricing of ads on digital platforms is not always a straightforward task, and Instagram is no different on this front. There are several factors that influence the cost of your ads and various ways of managing your budget accordingly.

Factors Influencing the Cost

The Instagram advertisement model is based on the CPC (cost per click) and CPM (cost per mille) methods, and the prices are determined by Instagram auctions. This data is obviously confidential. Even your target audience and the feedback on your ads have the potential to influence the advertisement costs.

According to AdEspresso's insight, which is based on monitoring $100 million worth of Instagram ad money spent in 2017, the average cost of CPC ads on the platform in the third quarter of the year ranged between $0.70 and $0.80. Please note that this is just a vague benchmark to give you a basic idea of the costs involved in Instagram advertising. These prices do vary based on the auction, location, audience, time of the day, day of the week, and so on.

How Can You Control Your Costs?

Seeing that ads that target a specific niche enjoy high rates of engagement, Instagram ads of this nature could end up costing you more than a similar campaign on Facebook. According to some advertisers, the cost of Instagram ads could be as high as $5 per CPM. The advertisers can decide how their ad budget is spent. You can either set a daily spending limit or set a lifetime budget and continue running the campaign for as long as the budget lasts. Advertisers can also control the ad schedule (specific time range during the day), ad delivery method (link clicks, unique daily reach, impressions), and the bid amount (manual or automatic).

How to Advertise on Instagram

Now that we have clearly established the marketing potential of Instagram advertising beyond any reasonable doubt, let's see how to set up your campaign. The good news is, if you are already familiar with the way advertising works on Facebook, then setting up Instagram ads is not a big deal at all. It is so easy that they can be configured through Facebook Ads Manager itself.

Are you already advertising on Facebook? If not, we'll walk you through the process of setting up Facebook Ads Manager so that you can run your Instagram ad campaign through it. It is to be noted that Instagram doesn't have its own ad manager, so you need to set up Facebook Ads Manager.

After logging into the appropriate Facebook account, navigate to its Ads Manager section, and determine your campaign goal. The interface is so intuitive that the goals are self-explanatory. The Instagram ads work for goals such as these:

• **Brand Awareness**

Simply select this option, then sit back and relax as Instagram works its magic to take your ads to potential users who are likely to be interested in your business. The platform is secretive about the logic and algorithm behind this campaign, but it does produce results as new and relevant users are exposed to your brand.

- **Traffic**

You can choose either to direct traffic to your website or to the app store where people can download your app. So, all you need to do is select one of these options under the "Traffic" menu and paste the relevant link there. There is not much else for you to do except to monitor the extent of traffic increase and gauge the effectiveness of your Instagram ad campaign.

- **Reach**

If you're looking to maximize the number of users that view your ads, then you need to first select your Instagram account before floating the ad campaign. You can take advantage of Facebook's Split Testing feature, which allows you to test two different ads to see which one leads to better results. If you are running an Instagram story ad, "Reach" is the only goal you can use for now.

- **Engagement**

Engagement is a great way to generate leads for your business; hence it is one of the most popular goals. However, unlike Facebook—where you can pay for "post engagements" or "event responses"—Instagram only allows you to pay for "post engagements" at present.

- **App Installs**

Setting up app installs as your goal is just as simple as selecting any other goal. All you need to do is select your app from the app store during setup.

- **Conversion**

This goal aims at leading your target audience to take action. This means using ads to drive users into purchasing something from your website or your app. In order to use this goal, you need to configure your Facebook Pixel, or an app event, based on your website or the app you're marketing. Once you finish this setup, you can keep track of the conversions.

- **Video Views**

The video views goal doesn't require any additional configuration or setup. Video content always requires you to invest a significant amount of time, money, effort, and creativity. It is always a good idea to pay to get more views for your content so that it can put you on the radar of a sizeable target audience.

Selecting the Target Audience

Once you have selected a suitable goal for your ad campaign, the next obvious step is to configure the type of audience to target. If you are already a Facebook advertiser, things will be very simple, as you will have different types of audience bases already selected. If you are not familiar with this, don't worry, it's not rocket science. Here is how you do it:

- **Location**

You can choose to target a specific country, state, region, city, zip code, or even exclude or include certain locations.

- **Age**

You can choose any age range from 13 years to over 65 years.

- **Gender**

You can target men, women, or all.

- **Languages**

If the language you are targeting is not common in your target location, it is better to leave this option blank. Even Facebook recommends the same.

- **Demographics**

This section, which falls under "Detailed Targeting," is powerful and offers detailed configuration settings. It has several multilayered subcategories that allow you to reach a specific niche. Just take enough time to explore all possible options to decide on the group of people to target.

- **Interests**

This also falls into the "Detailed Targeting" category. You can explore several subcategories to find users who are inclined to be interested in what you are promoting. For example, you can target users who like automobiles, travel, a specific genre of movies, and so on.

- **Behavior**

As you must have guessed it already, this also falls under the umbrella of "Detailed Targeting" and comes with seemingly limitless subcategories and options. You can select your target audience based on their purchasing behaviors, their jobs, anniversaries, and so on.

- **Connections**

This allows you to target users who are connected to your Instagram page, app, or event.

- **Custom Audience**

This needs a bit of preparatory effort on your part. It allows you to handpick your target audience and upload a list of contacts so that you can specifically reach the leads that are already in the bag. This option is also very helpful in reaching customers to pitch upselling.

- **Lookalike Audience**

If you are happy with the way your custom audience base is responding to your ad campaign, you can configure the Instagram ad to look for a "Lookalike Audience." This feature will find Instagram users possessing traits that are similar to your original custom audience base.

Once you're done configuring your target audience, Facebook Ads Manager will give you an idea of how specific or generic your audience base is. Too specific may limit your exposure, while too generic may dilute your ad campaign. You can reconfigure your target audience to strike a fine balance before you flag off the campaign.

Ad Placement

Other important points to take into consideration include determining the placements. If you leave it at "Automatic," the ad will end up running on both Facebook and Instagram. If you have created your ad content specifically for Instagram, then you should opt for "Edit Placement" and select "Instagram."

Budget and Schedule

If you're familiar with Google Ads, aka AdWords, the procedure is pretty much similar on Instagram. If you're new to the world of digital advertisements, then you have to implement a trial-and-error strategy to determine your ad schedule, daily budget, and lifetime budget.

Creating Instagram Ads

Once you've gone through all the above procedures, the only thing left for you to do is upload the ad content you've created and kick-start the campaign. Instagram ads can be created in the following formats: image feed, image story, video feed, video story, carousel images feed, and canvas story. Each has its technical requirements regarding size, memory, etc., and depending on the type of ad content, your available goal options may vary.

To conclude, Instagram advertising can be extremely productive for your brand or business. Being a multimedia platform, Instagram allows you to come up with great and creative ad content. Infuse your ad content with personality and contextual relevance, then watch the magic happen.

PART 3: INFLUENCER MARKETING

Chapter 11: What Are Influencers and Why Do You Need Them?

Recently, the term "influencer marketing" has gone viral. Considered to be one of the primary marketing strategies in today's social media scenarios, influencers are being hired on a massive scale to promote brands and drive sales. To begin with, the impact of influencers and influencer marketing wasn't so obvious. As more people joined social media platforms like Instagram and YouTube, it gave a boost to bloggers and influencers who started developing a strong fan base and following.

Instagram, among all platforms, has the highest engagement rate, with 3.2%, compared to 1.5% on other social media platforms. This engagement is also driven by the content produced by influencers.

How Do You Define Influencers?

Influencers are like mini-celebrities that literally have an "influence" on people. Every influencer has a specific language and niche within which they are instantly recognized. You can find influencers in all kinds of disciplines today, such as travel or fashion bloggers, journalists, photographers, and public speakers.

As more people joined social media over the past five to six years and started following people who give fashion, travel, fitness, makeup, and life advice, the term "influencer" was born. Marketers around the globe realized this impact that influencers had on their followers, which coined the term "influencer marketing." They started including it in their marketing plans instead of using the old-school, self-promotional strategies. The year 2017 alone witnessed 86% of marketers hiring influencers to promote their brand and drive more sales. The following three years saw a whopping 1,500% rise in the research for influencer marketing.

The world of Instagram has more than 500,000 influencers of all scales today.

What Are the Benefits of Hiring Influencers?

Massive Fan Following

Unless you plan on hiring micro-influencers, who have fewer followers than mega-influencers or world-famous celebrities, you have the major benefit of getting a massive number of potential customers. You will fetch a good number of followers, even if just a small percentage of viewers decide to follow your brand. If your products are promising, followers are bound to buy something at some point, turning it into an advantage in the long run. The fans also rely on influencers' suggestions. For instance, a study revealed that 33% of the Gen Z population who followed certain influencers relied on their decision to purchase a product.

People Trust Their Word

Since people follow these influencers because of their expert opinions and professional advice, they tend to trust everything they say. They somehow establish a friendly rapport with their fans that's informal and trustworthy. More than half of the influencers are authentic and stay true to their words, which is applauded by their followers. A lot of them are also considered to be role models for having established their own identity without depending on nepotism. Marketers take advantage of this trust, as well as the relationship between influencers and their followers, and pay influencers to promote their products. They depend on the fact that any information provided by these influencers is going to be received positively by their followers, which can lead to higher sales.

This type of indirect marketing also gives the consumers a chance to indulge in new products without facing the pressure to buy it, making it a nuanced marketing strategy that has a higher chance of success. Even though consumers are aware of the content being a sponsored endorsement, they still find the advice to be dependable and honest.

Highly Engaged Target Audience

Depending on the niche of certain influencers and their style, they can come with a highly engaged audience. Their followers take their advice and follow them for a reason. If your products or services are targeted to a certain group, you need to list the influencers you wish to collaborate with. For instance, if your company focuses on manufacturing skin products, you need to target the makeup and beauty bloggers within your area or country. In this case, your target audience will probably be the female population within an age range of 18 to 35 years old. This tactic will not only help you in reaching a major target audience but also in creating engagement, which can be very beneficial for your brand.

A great example of a brand that has solely relied on influencer marketing recently, without producing any commercials, is Daniel Wellington. The brand, which is a leading name in its discipline of designing watches, had to take this risk to understand better sales patterns and receive feedback from the audience.

Creative Way of Advertising Your Products

With so much content produced all over the platform every day, followers can get easily bored when they see repetitive posts. Even though it may look easy, it's highly challenging to keep your audience entertained with every post. There are many creative minds out there who put a lot of effort into creating excellent content, which can make the platform get saturated at some point. You can often find yourself brainstorming to be able to produce fresh content and failing to come up with new ideas.

That's when hiring influencers can help you. Influencers have their own style of producing content that is favored by their followers. They can promote your products in their own style and manner. This gives a different edge to your marketing, and your followers get to view fresh content, ultimately resulting in more engagement from old and new followers.

A Great Return on Investment

We've talked about the importance of the return on investment (ROI) while marketing on social media platforms. It takes a lot of effort, time, and money to produce content that can engage your audience. Influencers provide small brands and companies with great ROI, even with a fixed budget. Initially, it might seem expensive to pay hefty paychecks and give away freebies during contests held by your hired influencers. But as we discussed the impact of influencers on their followers, we can anticipate and calculate the ROI accordingly.

According to stats and numbers, you can expect to earn an average of $6.50 on every $1 spent, making it almost six times more beneficial. To have a successful return on investment, you just need to make a definite plan, determine your objectives, and set appropriate key performance indicators (KPIs). Also, it's important to define your main goal behind every campaign. Whether you need to boost engagement and increase your likes, shares, and comments, or you need to generate more sales, targeting influencers, and setting relevant strategies will help you tremendously.

Defining Micro- and Nano-Influencers

As the name suggests, micro- and nano-influencers are those who have a small number of followers compared to the bigger celebrities. However, they still have a major engagement with their followers.

Basically, these have 100,000 followers or less. With one-third of the channels belonging to micro-influencers with 10,000 to 100,000 followers, and only 1% being mega-influencers with more than 5 million followers, you can compare their relative and significant impact on the audience and benefit from it.

There's a marginal difference between the terms micro- and nano-influencers. The former has a follower count from 10,000 to 100,000, and the latter from 1,000 to 10,000. Micro-influencers have a better say and are driven to create content that hits the target, compared to nano-influencers. However, we're going to talk about both groups in a collective sense, given their high rate of engagement.

There are so many influencers on Instagram that selecting and hiring a particular bunch can get nerve-racking. Within this population, we'd recommend hiring micro-influencers and nano-influencers, rather than the major bloggers or Instagram celebrities, due to a number of reasons.

Here are some aspects of hiring micro-influencers for your marketing campaigns:

➤ Depending on their reach and number of followers, small-scale micro-influencers are either willing to exchange free products or demand a certain amount of money to promote your products. You need to target these influencers smartly depending on their fan base and demands, and most importantly, according to your budget.

➤ One great thing about micro-influencers is that they are usually quite open and genuine about their opinions. They obviously create amazing content; that's the very reason behind their popularity. Compared to mega-influencers, these people are more connected to their audience. That's because they can easily respond to every comment and private message, making people feel heard and important.

➤ According to statistics, they have a higher engagement and audience reach than bloggers who have more than 100,000 followers. In fact, it is twice or more than the other groups. This gives your brand the benefit of reaching a wider audience with an even higher engagement rate (coined as ER). According to a study conducted by HypeAuditor in January 2019 about the engagement rate within that year, it was found that influencers who had more than one million followers had an average engagement rate of 1.97%; those with 100,000 to one million followers had a 2.05% ER; 20,000 to 100,000 had a 2.15% ER; 5,000 to 20,000 had a 2.43% ER; 1,000 to 5,000 had a 5.60% ER. You can compare the impact of micro- and nano-influencers on the major bloggers by using this data.

➢ Micro-influencers tend to put more effort and time into creating quality content. They discover unseen aspects of your product and create content that's more specific to your category. Not only are their ads creative and unique, but you can also get a lot of notable feedback from their followers. Unlike the content posted on major channels where the feedback from customers often gets lost, the minor channels can give you access to every comment, private message, and insight from your potential customers.

➢ They rely on you, too. As we've mentioned before, a lot of micro-influencers agree to promote your brand and products only for a free supply of your products, instead of paychecks. This collaboration is helpful for both parties. They get to create new content, gather engagement, and receive free products. You, on the other hand, will benefit by saving a major amount of funding within your budget. Basically, they are cost-effective.

➢ Lastly, there is more reach and content creation with groups of micro-bloggers compared to major influencers. Instead of hiring just one or two mega-influencers who take up half of your budget plus the free products, you can target groups of micro-bloggers who will demand less money and generate more content. Instagram has 52% of bloggers who have 1,000 to 5,000 followers; 33.4% from 5,000 to 20,000; 8.2% from 20,000 to 100,000; 6% from 100,000 to 1 million, and only 0.3% of bloggers who have more than 1 million followers. This also increases your chances of running a few successful campaigns rather than one ineffective campaign with a single mega-influencer. Also, this results in more personalization and better targeting of the niche audience.

Influencer marketing is so prominent in this day and age that there are more and more rising influencers within various disciplines, trying their best to gain a solid following, going for collaborations that matter. This is also giving influencer marketing a major boost, which doesn't seem to be stopping any time soon.

Now that you're thoroughly introduced to influencers and the benefits of hiring them for marketing campaigns, let's delve into the influencer marketing process and the results you can expect from hiring nano-, micro-, and mega-influencers this year, in the following chapters.

Chapter 12: The Influencer Marketing Process

Now that we have seen who influencers are, how they can make a positive impact on your brand, and how the term "influencer marketing" came into being, let's take a step-by-step look at the marketing process involving them.

What Is Influencer Marketing?

To put it simply, influencer marketing involves associating your brand with suitable social media influencers who then market your brand to their followers. Naturally, for this to work, the influencers you associate with don't need to have a huge following on Instagram, but they should cater to your brand's niche. For example, using a widely followed influencer specializing in the apparel sector to promote your restaurant is not exactly a sound marketing strategy.

With the right kind of influencers, you can significantly enhance awareness of your brand, because their followers look up to them and usually trust their recommendations. It is reported that 92% of people would rather go with word-of-mouth recommendations by somebody they trust than blindly believe what the brands say. This makes influencers an important asset for your marketing campaign on social media, especially on Instagram.

Various small businesses have reported that influencer marketing is one the fastest ways of acquiring customers and that your ROI with this strategy can see more than a sixfold increase if done right. Of the businesses that are already working with influencers, 59% are planning on increasing their budget for influencer marketing.

Influencer marketing on Instagram can be used to raise your brand awareness, increase its popularity among target audiences, and drive conversions (increasing sales or inducing the users to take certain actions, such as visiting your website or subscribing to your service).

How to Find the Right Influencers for Your Campaign

The simplest way to find the right influencer on Instagram, who specializes in your niche, is by tracking them using relevant hashtags. You can also use various platforms like Statista, which constantly updates the top 10 list of best influencers on various social media platforms in domains like beauty, fashion, food, design, and travel.

Once you come up with a shortlist of influencers you want to engage with, it is always wise to perform some due diligence before contacting them and talking about a potential partnership. Sure, their content may look impactful, and their follower base may be huge, but there are a few aspects that need to be analyzed before getting them on board.

The brand fit and the authenticity of the influencer are very important, or else they will not be able to promote your brand in an honest and inspiring manner. It is also important to note how their content, imagery, and stance will align with your brand.

Of course, there is the matter of quantitative analysis of the influencer's profile. This involves various parameters like:

➢ Number of followers (translates into reach).

➢ Follower growth (speaks volumes about the influencer's ability to bring in new followers).

➢ Like - follower ratio (a measure of the influencer's engagement rate).

There is no point in hiring an influencer who has a huge number of followers without taking a few points into consideration:

➤ Followers may not care enough to engage with the influencer's posts.

➤ Daily follower changes (may indicate unsavory tactics like follower buying or follow-for-follow).

➤ Target group analysis (to deduct bots and fake followers).

➤ Outgoing mentions and posts (to check if the influencer is working with any of your rivals).

The concept of influencer marketing is getting so popular that several agencies aggregating the services of social media influencers have started cropping up around the world, such as Social Match, hi! share that, etc. These influencer marketing platforms act as matchmakers between the advertisers and influencers. They also act as mediators between the two parties and ensure that the whole transaction is fair for everyone involved. If you are new to the world of influencer marketing, approaching influencer marketing platforms to get things rolling is actually not a bad idea.

Approaching the Influencers

Once you've created your influencer shortlist, it's time to reach out to them and establish contact. You can start by following the influencers, engaging with their content, and then approaching them directly by asking for a quote. You can also ask them to review your products or offer to sponsor their initiatives related to your brand, in addition to being open to co-creating content with them. A good influencer will initiate their side of the relationship by trying to know more about your brand and what sort of role they can play in promoting it.

The product review or sponsored initiative would serve as an interview process for both parties. As a brand, you can gauge the influencer's ability to generate engagement with your brand, while the influencer will know whether his/her association with the brand is going to be fruitful in the long run or not.

A successful influencer is also one who receives collaboration requests from top brands on a daily basis. So, your proposal should stand out from the rest, and this means that you need to keep your first contact brief, simple, and to the point. Provide them with a brief description of your brand and its values, along with an outline of the planned campaign and its objectives. This is a good way to start. The time frame of your planned collaboration is also an important piece of information to communicate. If you manage to evoke a response from the influencer, it's time to share more info and highlight the strategy of your campaign.

Negotiating

Once you establish a conversation with a suitable influencer, the next step is to negotiate terms of cooperation. During this phase, it is important to talk about your expectations clearly, so that you can evaluate whether the influencer can help you achieve your goals.

Depending on the type of influencers you are engaging with, you may have to vary your incentives. For example, a micro-influencer in your niche may be content with a free product for review, whereas bigger influencers will have to be persuaded with large payments and even invitations to exclusive events.

One thing many influencers say is, "The advertisers have to give us something of value in order for us to work with them." Money is always welcome, but in several cases, depending on the nature of the collaboration, influencers also accept products or services in exchange for their promotional services. The bottom line is, you need to give the influencers something solid for them to accept your campaign proposal. Asking them to post a story with a discount on your product for their followers and promising them a marginal commission if they sell a product is a type of proposal well-established influencers steer clear of.

At the end of the day, influencers are human beings like the rest of us, and they shouldn't be treated as advertising media. So, communicating with a personal touch and taking a real interest in their personality will help the relationship-building process. This also makes price negotiation easier and more transparent.

Bringing Influencers on Board

Now that you're done negotiating the terms and conditions of the cooperation, it is time to get the influencer onboard. During this process, it is imperative to strike a fine balance between allowing the influencer to exercise his/her artistic freedom and ensuring that they respect certain specifications of the campaign to make it successful. Opting to co-create the content for the marketing campaign with your influencers is a nice way to blend their unique appeal with the authenticity of your brand.

The contract should include some aspects like campaign time frame and deadlines, required hashtags and tags, quantity of content and involved channels, required disclosure of paid cooperation (it's a matter of legality depending on your country), appearance and aesthetics of the content, tone adopted in the content, usage rights of the content under cooperation, exclusion of competitors in posting, and so on.

Campaign Execution

When the campaign sets sail, it is important to keep in constant touch with your influencers so as to keep tabs on the progress of your campaign. Being supportive of the influencers during the campaign and being open to their requests will help you build a strong relationship with your advertising partners. This constant monitoring will also give you valuable insights into the usefulness of your team of influencers. Who is difficult to work with? Who is easygoing? Who follows the preset guidelines the best?

Things to Do Post-Execution

Finally, you have finished running an advertisement campaign on Instagram using influencers. Things don't end here, because you have to determine the magnitude of success the whole operation has achieved. By reviewing KPIs and measuring the campaign outcome, you can determine how each influencer performed and how much value they have added to your campaign.

Depending on the nature of the campaign, KPIs may vary, but generic parameters include the follower growth on your Instagram channel (number of followers who came to your brand's account from that of the influencer), quantity of content under the cooperation, engagement (likes, comments, reposts), quality of comments, media value (the buzz the influencer managed to create around your brand), and mentions/tags.

The main objective of reviewing the campaign's effectiveness after the execution is to identify the room for improvement and to evaluate which influencer was successful and which one was not. This insight would greatly improve your success rate when it comes to future Instagram influencer advertising campaigns.

Retaining the Good Influencers

Just because you completed your campaign and have no plans to launch a new one in the immediate future, that doesn't mean you should disconnect from the good influencers who propelled your campaign toward success. Getting suitable influencers who can relate to your brand and its principles and add real value to your advertising campaign is easier said than done. That is exactly why you should try, by all means, to sustain the relationship with the right influencers that extend beyond the realms of a single ad campaign.

With the increasing popularity of Instagram's marketing potential, influencer marketing will continue to grow in importance for small, medium, and big businesses alike. Your business may be a small eatery in a humble city or a giant multi-national car manufacturer; you can always increase your marketing potential on Instagram by collaborating with the appropriate influencers and dishing out interesting and engaging ad campaigns.

Chapter 13: 5 Influencer Marketing Results to Expect

Even though we talked about the benefits of hiring influencers and the details of the process, we're now going to talk results, accompanied by important numbers and figures. Influencer marketing was such a big hit last year among all startups and small companies that around 90% of marketing agencies gave thumbs up to this brilliant marketing strategy. If you're just getting into a business and planning to promote it on Instagram, we'd highly recommend that you take a look at the numbers and apply them to your strategies accordingly.

Some Important Facts

Increasing Marketing Budget

Two-thirds of businesses on Instagram are planning to increase their marketing budget this year. Upon witnessing the rise of influencers and the success of influencer marketing over the past two years, 63% of marketers are willing to increase their budget to hire influencers to promote their products and brands. A staggering 98% of businesses who have already tapped into influencer marketing plan to keep the same budget or increase it in the year 2020.

Popular Influencer Niches

Among the several types of bloggers that are widely spread across various disciplines, certain niches are very popular among users. The influencers with the highest following seem to be in the entertainment business, with 47% of the total users making up their followers. Next in line are beauty bloggers and celebrities with 43% of users following; then fashion bloggers, having 39% of the total follower count.

Preferred Type of Content

While hiring influencers, you can talk to them about the content type they'd be producing, and you're expecting. A lot of influencers prefer producing videos and stories to images and text, as those sell more and are highly interactive. And for a good reason, 64% of users prefer watching videos, 61% prefer images, and only 38% prefer reading text content. Around 44% of followers prefer watching and interacting with live videos. Thus, when your influencer presents the draft about the content type, you can roughly expect the type of engagement you'd receive and tweak the content accordingly.

Discovering Products

Needless to say, the majority of the users who follow major and minor influencers find out about certain products through them. While 41% of consumers discover new brands and products weekly, 24% discover new products every day through influencers. On the other hand, consumers that find little to no new products or brands through influencers make up less than 1% of the followers. Statistics show that 87% of consumers tend to buy a product after being "influenced" by the influencer's recommendation.

Among many other stats and data, we're sure that these numbers would mark a few expectations that you should have after launching an influencer campaign.

What to Expect When Launching an Influencer Marketing Campaign

Once you've hired apt influencers depending on your category, target audience, and budget, you need to wait for at least two to four months before seeing the anticipated results. Patience is key here.

While you're drafting your campaign plan, you need to provide a time frame of three months before you actually start to see results. At times, you might also have to wait a bit longer, so be prepared for that.

Here, we'll present some basic approaches to outline and run a campaign, along with its rough timeline. Even though you've gone through a detailed explanation of the influencer marketing approach in the previous chapter, we'll point out the expectations behind each step and the thought processes that go into planning it.

This will give you an idea of a mockup campaign that would be useful once you begin, along with the results you can expect.

Prepare a Rough Draft for Your Campaign

This will include all the objectives and goals you'd want to achieve through your influencer campaign and the expectations you have from the influencers you've hired. We've discussed a few of these in the previous chapters, but let's dig deeper this time. Here are a few objectives that need to be outlined or expected from your campaign, among others.

Result 1: Increasing Brand Identity and Awareness in General

Since certain influencers stick to ethical causes and public awareness principles, their followers respect and trust every word they say. If you hire such influencers who will promote your brand, your company's name is bound to escalate with more and more people recognizing you and your products. As you know by now, they have a greater reach to the people in your niche audience, who are willing to follow the advice of their role models. Almost half of the total followers tend to follow an influencer's advice in buying products, including six out of ten teenagers on social media. Among all users, 86% of women rely on social media to find recommendations on items to buy.

Result 2: Driving Sales and Generating Revenue

One of the ultimate reasons to hire influencers is to drive sales and generate revenue. We're sure that this would be one of your main objectives, too. Spreading brand awareness isn't enough in itself. Since you're investing a lot of time and money in influencer marketing, you definitely want to boost your sales.

Result 3: Creatively Generated Content

At times, the content generated by influencers can be more creative than that of your own company's content creators and marketing agency. If that's the case, this specifically created content gets added to your creative campaign archives to stay recorded, and it can be reused in the future for further campaigns. This will basically result in user-generated content that can be shared across various social media platforms. Another interesting twist that can be included here is getting content from your followers. Basically, influencers can either hold contests or request their followers to create content using your products. This will not only lead to more sales, but you'll also have more content to post across your social media platforms.

Result 4: Increase in Return on Investment

Depending on their influencer marketing strategies, brands earn around $6.50 to $20 (usually the top 13% of brands) per $1 spent. The calculation for the ROI might seem challenging at first, but you'll slowly get the hang of it once you figure out the way. To adequately calculate the ROI, you can track the performance of each influencer by providing them with specific URLs that have respective discount codes and request insights into the driven traffic. Next, you need to define specific key performance indicators (KPIs) per influencer to understand the engagement, traffic, interaction, and conversions that their content has generated. You can also use some external tools that can easily calculate the probable return on investment and determine whether you'll reach your goals or not.

Result 5: Keeping the Brand Real and Transparent

A lot of brands worry about losing authenticity when it comes to influencer marketing. Most of the influencers are honest and clear in voicing their opinions. However, there are a few bloggers out there who either provide false information or are just asset-driven. A lot of users on Instagram believe that, too. This leads to a fear of losing authenticity among brands. By doing some thorough research and being aware of the influencers you're interested in hiring, you can avoid this. Since most of the followers are already relying on the opinions of certain influencers, you don't have to worry about losing the brand's transparency.

Choose and Recruit Influencers Wisely

Choosing the right influencers for this job is a crucial step to gain the expected results. You can consider these three factors to choose an appropriate group of influencers for your campaign:

1. Know Your Niche and Target Audience

Even though this might sound repetitive, you really need to choose influencers that have a specific target audience to cater to their interests. For instance, hiring a makeup blogger to promote baby products doesn't make sense. Your target audience should be mothers and women in the 30 – 45 age group as opposed to a group of younger women. You should target the group that would actually be interested in your products. Research the influencers within your reach and location, shortlist them accordingly, and then narrow down your choices.

2. Evaluate the Engagement Rate

Depending on their reach, engagement rate, and type of content, every influencer has a different rate of reach and engagement. We saw the numbers in the earlier chapters. At times, it's possible that certain influencers might have more followers but less engagement, but a few might have half the followers and more engagement. In this case, you need to compare the numbers and ratios and choose accordingly. Here, you're expecting a higher engagement rate and more followers depending on the ER of your influencer.

3. Consider Your Budget

You're well aware of the budget perspective involved in influencer marketing. But we're just mentioning it here so that you know what to expect from it and avoid making mistakes. First, you're definitely not supposed to overshoot your budget by hiring an influencer that is overcharging for a certain campaign. There are always better options out there; just be aware of them and do your research. You might want to consider hiring micro- or nano-influencers, as you know the benefits of hiring them by now.

Launch the Campaign and Compare the Results

When you have it all prepared, you're ready to launch the campaign and wait for your influencers to create content and promote it according to the chosen time frame (probably around three to five weeks on average). And as mentioned, wait for at least two to four months. After the waiting period is over, look at, and reflect on the results. It is, however, not advised to compare the results of every influencer you've hired to one another, as they tend to function differently.

These influencer marketing strategies and the results they yield are surely intriguing. It would be a great idea to tap into them this year, as the future seems quite bright. Speaking of the future, it's time to learn more about what 2020 holds when it comes to influencer marketing and the possible scenarios it has in store for your brand.

Chapter 14: The Future of Influencer Marketing

We're sure that you're entirely familiar with influencers, the benefits of hiring them, and their marketing process by now. To end this insightful section, let's discuss what this strategy holds for you in the future. Steadily carving its path to becoming a whopping $8-billion industry this year, influencer marketing is here to stay. So much so that skeptics who initially denied the growth of influencer marketing are now agreeing to the massive jump and success of this market. It is, in fact, predicted to jump up to $10 billion by the year 2022, which is a very short gap for such a big margin.

As we've mentioned before, a majority of brands are keeping the same budget or planning on increasing it this year. A notable example is the brand Estee Lauder. It is planning to channel 75% of its marketing and advertising budget into influencer marketing. Brands are starting to realize the importance of this industry.

Here are a few predictions about influencer marketing that you need to keep in mind. A few of them can also boom as major trends that brands might follow. You're here at the right time; just make a note of these before they go big.

Trend 1: Nano-Influencers Will Take the Spotlight

Even though we defined the various categories of influencers in the earlier chapters, let's present it in a more detailed manner for a better understanding. The five main types of influencers are nano-influencers with 1,000 to 10,000 followers, micro-influencers with 10,000 to 50,000 followers, mid-tier influencers with 50,000 to 500,000 followers, macro-influencers with 500,000 to 1 million followers, and mega-influencers with 1 million followers and more. Until now, brands have majorly hired macro- and mega-influencers due to their higher fan following. However, marketing agencies are starting to realize the importance of nano-influencers.

These bring in amazing ROI through high engagement with a very small investment. We have already talked about the benefits of hiring nano- and micro-influencers, and you can see why we're emphasizing it again. Brands have started their search for nano-influencers who can make a bigger difference with a higher interaction rate compared to the bigger investment and a lower interaction rate in proportion. Also, the quality of content is reliable with these small-scale influencers. So, all in all, the predicted trend this year might be hiring a bunch of nano-influencers that don't burn a hole in your pocket, instead of one or two mega-influencers that pose a higher risk of failure.

Trend 2: Mega-Influencers Will Launch Their Own Lines

Already seeing progress, this trend will continue to evolve further this year. Brands are slowly taking steps toward approaching influencers to collaborate and launch products in their names. Even though brands have to allocate a massive budget to this practice, they are prepared to do this due to the predicted success rate. This is a major step up from hiring influencers one by one. Not only is it a major capitalization move, but also a massive risk to completely launch a new line. It can either be a huge success or a complete disaster.

Well, as per the past experiments, this move has witnessed a massive success. The use of influencers to launch either a significant makeup or clothing line has turned followers into potential customers, driving huge leads, and generating revenue. Influencers are also seeking the shelter of major brands to launch their own lines. They act as the main face of the launch and are successful in influencing the younger demographics. Whichever way it goes, this intriguing collaboration can be predicted to be one of the *greatest* shifts that will be majorly carried out by marketing agencies this year.

Trend 3: There Will Be Events Specifically Held for Influencers

There have already been a few influencer events over the past two years where important influencers of various scales are gathered and awarded with specifically categorized nominations. These work the same way as the big events that are held for mega-celebrities. This trend is expected to grow this year. A number of brands are coming together and sponsoring such events to put a spotlight on their influencers. This will also help them in their campaigns and generate more brand awareness. It can be an awards show, a cocktail party, an informal gathering, or even a trip to a foreign country.

These influencers would either require a special invitation or act as the face for the brand. They contribute by shooting photos or videos containing special moments of the event or trip, and posting them regularly on their social media channels. This provides the brand with even more recognition. One great example of this is the brand Revolve, which sends special invitations to top-level influencers for events like Coachella. There were many stories, images, and videos produced, and the brand got a lot of recognition and engagement this way. This trend seems to be continuing this year, and probably will keep on evolving further, as well.

Trend 4: Influencer Marketing Will Become a Mandatory Strategy

Traditional advertising methods are already less engaging in today's digitally interactive world. Influencer marketing is proven to be one of the top interaction-building strategies, which can create engagement and turn likes and shares into leads. While marketing agencies are experimenting with different influencers and comparing results, they are increasingly planning on keeping the strategy permanent due to its massive success. It is possible to see a lot of brands continuously promoting their products with the help of influencers. So much so that a few brands are signing long-term contracts with select influencers. The reasons behind this are simple. These people are easy to approach and work with and can create more interaction and engagement than high-end celebrities.

This is also because of the relationship that influencers have with their followers. As we discussed, their followers tend to take their advice and recommendations seriously, and the majority of their audience relies on them when buying certain products. It has also gotten a lot easier for marketers to calculate the return on investment. They are able to establish better contracts and have a better understanding of the process.

Trend 5: There Will Be Stricter Regulations and Enforcement

There are speculations of stricter rules being imposed on influencers that plan on collaborating with any brand. The FTC (Federal Trade Commission) announced that they need to be informed about any plausible collaboration between brands and influencers. It was initially taken very lightly by bloggers all across the platform, but they are now slowly becoming more aware and careful about it. Also known as FTC's Influencer Guidelines, these regulations are put forward to avoid unmarked sponsorships and false agreements between two parties. These rules are also framed to avoid fake advertisements that users often encounter on the platform.

The guidelines also mention highlighting the agreement between the influencer and the brand to keep the collaboration transparent and authentic. It can either be done by marking it within your content to make it visible or mentioning it in your videos. However, these also waive off the need to disclose the agreement through hashtags, which was actually not preferred by the influencers. When these rules weren't so prominent earlier, and not many influencers took them seriously, marketing agencies also shunned them. But with the growth of this market, the regulations are expected to get stricter this year.

Trend 6: More Video Content and Podcasts

We've mentioned it over and over again, but we can't highlight the importance of video content enough. It is going to evolve further this year. Podcasts are gaining a lot of popularity because a lot of followers are keen on hearing and being "influenced" by their favorite bloggers. And as the bandwidth and internet services are improving, more video and audio content is being produced and easily accessed. As we saw that a majority of users (6 out of 10) prefer watching videos instead of watching television, more than 80% of businesses and marketing agencies are now getting into this type of content.

Even though YouTube is highly preferred for video and audio content, the advent of Instagram stories and IGTV videos has increased the caliber and opportunity to create videos on this social media platform. This is a great way of creating interaction and engagement. There were around 29 million podcast episodes and about 700,000 podcasts running actively at the end of 2019. This number is only going to rise steadily this year. And while 51% of the US population has listened to—or prefers to listen to—a podcast episode, you can definitely note it as a great strategy to incorporate into your plan.

There's no stopping influencer marketing this year; it's only going to evolve further in the coming years—unless there is no social media, which, of course, is highly unlikely. Catch up with these trends before they become common, too. It isn't as difficult as it sounds. Just make a detailed plan and follow it in order to know all the potential risks and pitfalls. Even if you fail, there's a valuable lesson for you there.

That said, we're sure that you're now thoroughly prepared to stand out from the crowd and win the Instagram marketing game. Since everyone is creating their niche on this massive social media platform, it is time for you to roll up your sleeves and carve your own path to success. As you've seen time and again in this book, it's not rocket science. You just need to be creative, pay attention to the unseen factors, create a contingency plan, and follow it consistently. Good luck!

Check out another book by Chase Barlow

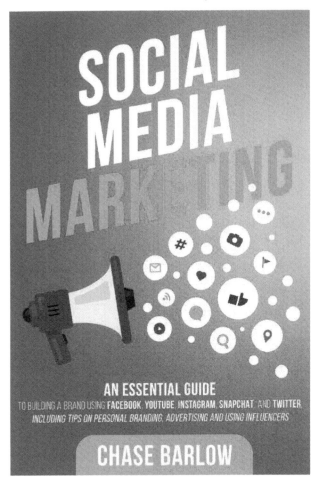

Resources

https://www.makeuseof.com/tag/what-is-instagram-how-does-instagram-work/

https://www.lyfemarketing.com/blog/why-use-instagram/

https://elisedarma.com/blog/why-instagram-best-platform

https://blog.hootsuite.com/instagram-statistics/

https://www.techuntold.com/instagram-pros-cons/

https://www.yrcharisma.com/2019/10/22/pros-and-cons-of-instagram-business-profile/

https://suebzimmerman.com/a-beginners-guide-to-getting-started-on-instagram-in-2019/

https://www.youtube.com/watch?v=6_qfwSMo_Js,

https://www.youtube.com/watch?v=K3cY_AGDBgU,

https://www.youtube.com/watch?v=o_q02EtWsUc

https://later.com/blog/ultimate-guide-to-using-instagram-hashtags/,

https://www.youtube.com/watch?v=I3uxif_AIFk,

https://www.youtube.com/watch?v=8JbDFbqguxo,

https://later.com/training/instagram-stories-small-business/,

https://smallbiztrends.com/2019/05/instagram-stories-tips.html

https://www.youtube.com/watch?v=ZfzaLQKXVpg,

https://www.youtube.com/watch?v=d8U01W3DIG0,

https://www.youtube.com/watch?v=B2VxC4v_nxA,

https://www.youtube.com/watch?v=dvEQiuBDSVA,
https://thenextscoop.com/instagram-video-marketing/,
https://www.jennstrends.com/drive-traffic-with-instagram/
https://www.oberlo.com/blog/instagram-shopping,
https://www.youtube.com/watch?v=k0Oe64_eS3Y
https://www.wordstream.com/blog/ws/2017/11/20/instagram-advertising,   https://www.youtube.com/watch?v=ePOJhIx8gOo&t=18s,
https://www.youtube.com/watch?v=ta8dmGzI50M
https://shanebarker.com/blog/rise-of-influencer-marketing/,
https://later.com/blog/instagram-influencer-marketing/,
https://mention.com/en/blog/influencer-marketing-as-a-small-business-owner/,
https://www.jeffbullas.com/influencer-marketing-for-small-business/
https://www.grouphigh.com/blog/small-business-guide-beginning-influencer-marketing/,   https://influencerdb.com/blog/9-steps-influencer-marketing-process/,
https://www.allbusiness.com/work-with-influencers-102360-1.html,
https://blog.perlu.com/how-to-do-influencer-marketing/
https://izea.com/influencer-marketing-statistics/,
https://www.seoblog.com/3-types-roi-expect-influencer-marketing/
https://www.socialmediatoday.com/news/why-the-future-of-influencer-marketing-will-be-organic-influencers/567463/,
https://shanebarker.com/blog/future-of-influencer-marketing/?doing_wp_cron=1577632008.8945600986480712890625

Printed in Great Britain
by Amazon